Armchair Assessments:

Existing as a Detroit Lions Fan

Mark McCarthy

For information about this title or to order other books
and/or electronic media, contact the publisher:

Two Sisters Writing & Publishing®
TwoSistersWriting.com
18530 Mack Avenue, Suite 166
Grosse Pointe Farms, MI 48236

Paperback ISBN: 978-1-956879-80-3
Ebook ISBN: 978-1-956879-81-0

Printed in the United States of America

No part of this manuscript is fiction.

Book cover design and interior formatting: Van-Garde Imagery, Inc.

Author photos: The McCarthy Family Collection.

Dedication

THIS STORY IS DEDICATED to my nephew, Michael. I miss you, and wish I had been able to spend much more of your time on earth together. Life does not always allow our wants and needs to be fulfilled.

To be certain, the Lions do not "stink" anymore. However, everything is fleeting, and can change in the bat of an eyelash. Your departure remains a stark reminder of that reality. I hope that you are looking down, shining your light on your family, and continuing to protect all of us. I hope to be chosen to join you again someday, and simply catch up, on what was missed between us.

Continue to rest in peace, Sotsie.

Contents

Chapter 1

Baptism

WHAT WOULD ONE BEST describe as a "miracle of nature?" It is certainly a subjective term. One definition is presented as an extraordinary event that is inexplicable by natural laws, but happens in a natural way. I wholeheartedly agree with this definition, and these three words will explain why, while also answering the original question: the Detroit Lions.

I would argue that the Lions are the most snakebitten in all of major sports teams in history. Without question, many of the wounds that they have suffered over the years have been self-inflicted, but many others had causes that are more difficult to fathom.

My introduction to the Lions began at an early age. My father was a drinker and a gambler, skilled at the former, woefully inefficient at the latter. I vividly remember him cursing at the television at the bar where he spent "quality time" with me. His venom was squarely aimed at the Lions. As it turns out, a trend had emerged in his gambling: when he wagered in favor of the home team, they would lose. If he decided to bet against them, they would somehow emerge victorious. It drove him insane.

I will never forget these foreboding words he spoke to me: "Son, do not EVER… become a Lions fan."

I am hopeful that, in my life, I will be rewarded just once while forgoing that "advice."

I knew nothing of the Lions until I was six years old, on the 24th of October, 1971. On that day, the Lions' wide receiver Chuck Hughes collapsed and died on the field. It was late in the game, with just over a minute remaining, and as of 2024, he still remains the ONLY player to lose his life while playing. I did not witness the tragic event. I simply remember my father talking about it with other patrons of the bar. Morbid curiosity had taken over.

Often, the word "only" is highlighted in these writings, emphasizing the Lions' many lowlights. I earnestly wish not to mock the misfortune that the Lions have endured, on and off the field, but maintaining a sense of humor has been an integral mechanism for getting through the decades of almost constant failure. Football is akin to religion in the city of Detroit, and I readily admit that Ford Field has been my house of worship for eight Sunday afternoons every Fall. My football heart bleeds Honolulu Blue. However, history tells a story of incredible letdowns, inexplicable defeats, and simply… heartbreak.

I have watched every snap of Lions football for more than 40 years. It has not been easy. In anticipation of the hope each new season brings, the Lions pride "eats the cornbread" (hot out of the oven) and drinks the "Kool Aid." Honolulu Blue flavor, of course.

My best analogy is to describe my loyalty as a hopeless drug habit: not good for my health or my wallet, and it inevitably extends into my personal life and relationships. And no, I have never had any such addiction.

My hygienist suggested to me that perhaps the Lions are the ones with the addiction, and that I play the role of the enabler. They resist the temptation for a while, giving me just enough hope, showing a bit of promise, only for them to return to their destructive ways and disappoint me. I appreciate the lifeline that she was trying to offer me, but no. I am the one with the compulsion...

I don't pay attention to how others interpret the Lions; I never bother to break down an injury report, for example, nor am I swayed by the "hot take" of a TV analyst. I merely watch closely as the Lions play, trusting my own two eyes. My hope is to use my observations to provide a unique perspective of this franchise and what investing in it has done, not only to myself, but to a very large and passionate fanbase. I want to let the world know what all of us Lions fans have been through, through my own lens. I could never endeavor to recall every single one of the truly shocking follies that I have witnessed. A truck would be necessary to haul away the weight of them, and I own a sedan. Much of what I've witnessed is buried in the dark recesses of my mind, to the point where I actually want, and NEED, to forget some of them.

A bit of a precursor, if I may? Let me crack the door and provide a glimpse inside the purgatory. The Lions hold the record for the longest consecutive road losing streak in league history—26 games, attained from 2007 to 2010. Similarly, their longest road losing streak against the SAME opponent, the Green Bay Packers, lasted for 24 years, beginning in 1991, until 2015. One of which was a playoff game. Yes, they went zero for the state of Wisconsin for 24 years, when visiting the Packers. This is a truly incredible number of losses, especially when you consider that the Lions play there every season.

However, they broke their streak against the Packers in customary Lions fashion, as I knew they would: the Packers drove for a long touchdown, cutting the lead to 18–16, with 32 seconds remaining. The two-point conversion attempt failed, preserving the lead. The only formality that remained was the impending onside kick attempt by the Packers. This was a longshot at best. But longshots are always a possibility when trying to achieve a minor miracle against my Lions. The bouncing kick was bobbled by a Lions player, and Green Bay recovered the ball. In the 2015 season, there were a total of 66 onside kicks attempted, and a grand total of nine were successfully recovered. Nine. Just warming the engine up! After the recovery, the Packers drove into field goal range, only to lose the game when Mason Crosby missed a 52-yard attempt, as time expired.

The Lions have often had matters in hand, given control away in grand fashion, and then survived on dumb luck. That usually has been their script, at least when they manage to end up on the winning side. And what did it amount to, when they finally broke their losing streak? Absolutely nothing. The win improved their record to 2–7.

Many Sundays of my life have been spent deciding between the "honey do list" or three hours of consternation. Taking my current single status into consideration, it leaves me wondering if I made the correct choice. Yes, I actually think I did!

Going over losses, coaching decisions, plays that were botched, and other variables that have contributed to the Lions' reputation are all itemized examples of what I wish "could have been different," even long after time has passed. The ridicule I receive for supporting the Lions always comes my way, and what else can I do, except... accept it? It is not as though I have any ammunition with which to make a presentable argument. Still, I continue to advocate for them, regardless. I always look ahead to each season, hoping that the upcoming one will be the blind squirrel finding the acorn. But… I also temper my expectations, by never forgetting who and what they have been.

Am I loyal, or simply foolish? With my personal life squared away, I figure that I can stand to dredge up a fair amount of drama and dysfunction. The Lions provide that in spades. Once, I was with my brother for a road game. It was the Los Angeles Rams vs. the Lions in 2021. I had to show a COVID vaccination card for entry. The only reason I took the shot was for this event. Thanks for that, California Governor Gavin Newsome. Still… family, football, and good times. Exactly what life should be about, agreed? Detroit scored quickly on a long touchdown pass, early in the game. I didn't celebrate yet; my eyes were scouring the field for something else.

After my brother applauded the play, he glanced over at me and asked, "What are you looking at?"

I replied, "I am trying to see if there is a flag on the Lions."

THIS is an example of what they have done to me. They lost the game, to drop to 0-7.

The moments that I will share with you are so much more to me than just rehash. They are flashbacks, and the details are what make the Lions truly one of a kind. Often, I have wondered why there has not been a video documentary produced about the Lions, chronicling their history. For sports fans, it would be eye-opening. In the absence of such a production, I will attempt to paint as vivid of a picture as possible. Please keep in mind that my opinions are simply that—opinions. Are you strapped in, ready to take that stroll down memory lane with me? Let's reminisce…

Chapter 2

A Curse?

IN 1958, THE LIONS traded their star quarterback, Bobby Layne, to the Pittsburgh Steelers. This was done just two games into the season. Rumors varied as to why the move was made, and Layne's off-field behaviors were frequently mentioned as being a large part of the reason: gambling, drinking, etc. Despite his flaws, he led the Detroit franchise to titles in 1952, 1953, and as recently as in the previous 1957 season, which still remains their last, even today. Without question, Layne was one of the most talented players in the league. In the trade, the Lions acquired quarterback Earl Morral and two draft choices.

Upon leaving the locker room for the last time, Layne reportedly (and angrily) stated that the team would not win again for 50 years. With those words, what began is affectionally known in Motown as "The Curse of Bobby Layne."[1]

No titles for 50 years, you said, Mr. Layne? I truly wish you had been correct. It has now far surpassed five decades: it's been 66 years, to be more exact.

A curse, you say? Typically, I would never subscribe to such a notion. I am calm, measured, and rational. However, based on what all of us have witnessed of the Lions in our lifetime, allow me to query that theory. I already mentioned the tragedy involving Chuck Hughes. Eerily similar instances are as follows: on June 6th, 1992, the Lions' offensive Lineman, Eric Andolsek, was killed when a driver of a semi-truck ran off the road and struck him, while he was working on his lawn in Louisiana. ON HIS LAWN!! Unthinkable, and again… tragic.

The trend continues: on November 17th, 1991, another Lions' offensive lineman, Mike Utley, was injured while blocking on the first play of the fourth quarter, against the Los Angeles Rams. He suffered a cervical vertebrae injury, leaving him paralyzed from the chest down.

I was at that game, and I remember every moment, from the hushed devastation that the crowd shared, to the jubilation when he was carried from the field, giving all of us a thumbs-up as he went. It was uplifting, but also ironic, that one of most emotional moments that Lions fans have experienced was associated with disaster instead of triumph. But it can be no other way. THAT is what I am trying to impart to you.

The Mike Utley Foundation was created the year after his injury, and it continues to operate today, searching for a cure for spinal injuries while supporting and rehabilitating those who have suffered the same. Thank you, Mr. Utley, for turning tragedy into bravery, and for helping to change the lives of those who have suffered catastrophic circumstances. You are a hero to many, myself included.

Allow me to switch lanes. Or veer into a "Lions only" alley of sorts. On December 21st, 1997, against the New York Jets, Barry Sanders rushed for 184 yards, and totaled 2,053 yards for the season. At the time, he was only the third player in league history to run for more than 2,000 yards in a season. What negative connotation could possibly be associated with such a tremendous feat? Leave that answer to Lions lore: on the very same day, in the exact same game, tragedy struck again. Yes, another disaster. Lions linebacker Reggie Brown fell unconscious on the Silverdome turf, after what appeared to be a routine play, much like the Mike Utley play. Both occurrences happened in the fourth quarter. Brown's helmet made contact with a Jets lineman, who was blocking on the play, as he fell to the ground. He, like Utley, suffered a spinal cord injury.

As with the Utley injury, I also witnessed Brown's injury, having attended both games. The mood was much more somber when Brown was taken from the field, because of the obvious uncertainty: unlike Utley and his famous thumbs-up, Brown never moved as he was taken away. It was unclear whether he would ever recover.

Over the course of two weeks, he was able to stand and he began to walk again. Soon after, a news conference was hosted to give him the opportunity to update fans about his status, his rehab journey, etc. He did just that: Brown rose from a wheelchair and walked without assistance to the podium. An incredible and inspiring moment. I can only think of a small handful of Lions players who immediately stood out and performed as advertised, as soon as they took the field. Reggie Brown is undoubtedly one of those.

When I watched him walk on his own after his injury, it gave me more satisfaction than any Lions win ever could. Thank you, brother, for being a Detroit Lion. You were a great player to watch.

Two devastating, unthinkable on-field tragedies, along with another off the field, when a guy was simply tending to his yard. Have such personal afflictions ever been "bestowed" upon other teams? I am certainly unaware of any such phenomenon.

In 1991, during the season of Mike Utley's injury, the Lions won their only playoff game since 1957 against the Dallas Cowboys. And in 1997, during Reggie Brown's injury season, Barry Sanders reached a personal milestone, and the Lions earned a playoff berth. The point being, even when the Lions enjoy a modicum of success within a calendar year, it is always accompanied with historical misfortune, both on and off the field. Did Bobby Layne have an epiphany on that day in 1958?

Chapter 3

Do Numbers Lie?

IT'S A VERY VALID question. The NFL calculates a mountain of data on each of its teams, which is used to rank each team's performance in various categories. These include offensive and defensive performance, as well as the performance of their special teams, etc. All of this data contributes to each team's ranking, which are all then compared with other teams in the NFL Power Ranking system. Every team's rank is updated each in-season week.

So is the system trustworthy? Are those numbers telling us the truth? It can be hard to tell, until you look closer at the statistics behind each ranking. Here is an example. A team ranks first in the league in pass defense. Simply meaning, they give up the least amount of passing yardage. Sounds straightforward, wouldn't you agree? Here is where that number becomes skewed: because said team is so poor at defending the RUN, the number of passing attempts that the opponent strives for diminishes, which keeps the statistic of the first-ranked pass defense lower, and "better" on paper only. Why attempt to pass frequently, when you can focus mainly on their rushing defense?

Therefore, in this example, numbers do lie, or they at least fail to tell the whole story. In other occurrences, however, the sledgehammer drops, and you can feel how sobering numbers can be. Here are some that leave no doubt in my mind whatsoever.

All of the following applies prior to January 13th, 2024.
The Lions had not won a playoff game since January 5th, 1992. It was the longest such streak in the league. Yes, just north of 32 years. To be more exact, 11,696 days. Please, do not ask if that includes leap years! The world has changed quite a bit since then. In 1992, the cost for a gallon of gas was around $1.15. Bill Clinton became the President of the United States.

The Lions clinched the division title on Christmas Eve, 2023. Why so positive, you may wonder? With any good, Lions absurdity has never been far behind. It was their first division title in 30 years. Yes, since 1993. It was also the longest streak of that kind in the league. When they last won their division, it was named the NFC Central. It is now the NFC North. Nine straight playoff losses since 1993. Also a league worst during that span. They were the first NON-EXPANSION team to go winless in a season since World War II.

This abhorrent distinction was accomplished while going 0-16 during the 2008 season. In their inaugural season of 1976, the Tampa Bay Buccaneers went winless, when the NFL played only 14 regular season games. Not to be outdone, the Lions were the first to go winless after the league switched to a 16-game regular season in 1978. Comparing the Lions with the worst of the worst, there are six teams with a LOWER all-time winning percentage. However, the following resumes are far superior to that of the Lions.

Again, these numbers apply as of, and prior to, January 13th, 2024.

1) New York Jets—12 all-time playoff wins, four division titles (two in the NFL, and two AFL) and a Super Bowl win.

2) Atlanta Falcons—A Super Bowl appearance, four division titles, and 10 playoff wins.

3) Houston Texans—Seven division titles and five playoff wins. And they have only been an NFL franchise since 2002.

4) Arizona/St. Louis Cardinals—A Super Bowl appearance, three division titles, and five playoff wins since moving to Arizona, beginning in the 1988 season.

5) Jacksonville Jaguars—Eight playoff wins, four division titles, only having joined the league in 1995.

6) Tampa Bay Buccaneers—Yes, the same team that went winless in their first season. They have the lowest winning percentage of any team of all time, by a wide margin. They also have won two Super Bowls, nine division titles, and have 11 total playoff wins. All of these accolades earned since 1976. Simply mind blowing. Add their 12th playoff win on January 15th, 2024. (Monday Night Football playoff game.)

There are only four teams that have never reached the Super Bowl. Cleveland, Houston, and Jacksonville are three of them. Take a wild guess who the other is…

In the realm of sports fandom, which city has suffered the most misfortunes and failures on behalf of its team, over a period of time that spans a lifetime for most? Some would make a case for the Chicago Cubs. Yes, they waited 108 years before winning their World Series title in 2016, but had numerous other playoff appearances and series wins throughout the 80s, 90s, 2000s, and as recently as 2020. So, cross them off the list. The Boston Red Sox? Not even close. They waited 86 years, afflicted by "the curse of the Bambino" until 2004, when they won their own World Series. And they did it in grand fashion, erasing a 3–0 series deficit in the American League championship series against the New York Yankees. They remain the only team in MLB history to overcome that deficit. Soon thereafter, they won additional World Series titles in 2007, 2013, and 2018.

So, no. Not Boston. The closest comparison? For my money, that would be the Cleveland Browns. The franchise was moved from Cleveland to Baltimore in 1996. Not having a home football team to watch on fall Sundays would be gut-wrenching, for sure. A new franchise arrived in Cleveland, in 1999. In 1986 and 1987, the Browns lost consecutive AFC title games to the Denver Broncos. In the first game, played in January of 1987 (1986 season), they fell victim to what is now known as "The Drive": a 98-yard, five-minute methodical march in the freezing cold, led by John Elway. The Broncos tied the game with 37 seconds remaining in regulation, and they won in overtime.

In January of 1988 (1987 season), the Browns and Broncos were matched up again, with a trip to the Super Bowl again on the line. With the Browns driving for a tying touchdown late in the game, running back Earnest Byner took a handoff at the Denver eight-yard line, fumbled, and the Broncos recovered at the three-yard line, effectively ending the game. This unfortunate gaffe is referred to in NFL annals as "The Fumble." Pure heartbreak, two years in a row. Tough to imagine. Throw in a winless season of their own in 2017, and yes, the Cleveland faithful have had it rough. Still, the old franchise (prior to 1996) had six division titles, and four playoff wins. Add another win by the "New" Browns in the playoffs in 2020, and their resume is still preferable to that of the Lions. And devoid of any personal tragedies to a player. Yes, Browns fans, you have seen a lot of misfortune. But take solace, fellow Lions fans. The late and great Prince said it best by crooning: "Nothing Compares 2 U."

Chapter 4

Odds and Ends

THE LIONS' ALL-TIME LEADING scorer is a kicker named Jason Hanson, who played from 1992 until 2012. And the all-time winningest coach? That would be one Wayne Fontes, with 66 regular season wins from 1988 to 1996. It was great to see him make an appearance at Ford Field during the 2023 season. The crowd loved it, and so did I.

In the midst of their winless 2008 season, quarterback Dan Orlovsky took a snap in the end zone, and he ran out of the back of it for a safety. He wasn't forced out, or tackled. He simply did not know where the end line was. The play itself, and his career as a Lion, hold virtually no significance; it was just comical to watch.

Staying in the "perfect" 2008 season, during the season opener, the Lions faced off against the Atlanta Falcons. The Falcons' quarterback Matt Ryan threw his first-ever pass in his professional career, and it was a 62-yard touchdown, ultimately beating the Lions 34–21. Perhaps this was a precursor for the historical disaster that the 2008 campaign became? Yes, without question.

Which team do you think has the shortest regular season overtime loss in league history? That honor belongs to... you guessed it. The Chicago Bears' Dave Williams took the kickoff and returned it 95 yards on Thanksgiving Day, 1980, in 13 seconds. Another holiday gift to us, from the Lions. As if the abrupt ending was not enough, Chicago overcame a two-touchdown deficit in the fourth quarter, which included a score on the last play in regulation, which forced the overtime.

Let's see. What else? Go ahead and spin the wheel… Ah, yes. I remember. On December 30th, 1995, the Lions lost a playoff game to the Philadelphia Eagles. Just another common occurrence? Not exactly. It is still the highest-scoring regulation game in NFL playoff history. The final score was 58–37. Yes, a lopsided score. However, the contest was not that "close." At one point in the game, the score was 51–7. Mind boggling. The quarterback for the Eagles on that day? Prepare the wound for a bit more salt… Rodney Peete, the ex-Detroit Lion.

On November 8th, 1970, the New Orleans Saints' kicker Tom Dempsey kicked an NFL then-record 63-yard field goal to defeat the Lions. And of course, this happened right as time expired. Kicks of that distance were unheard of in that era of football. In this day and age, they have become much more common, with games being played indoors, and the kickers themselves being stronger and better athletes. Even more incredible, is that Dempsey was born with only half of his right foot.

On September 26th, 2021, our hometown heroes outdid themselves, once again. Justin Tucker of the Baltimore Ravens kicked a now NFL record 66-yard field goal, to beat the Lions. The ball barely made it to the crossbar, bounced straight up, and then barely cleared the bar on its descent. A truly miraculous sequence of events. And of course, this also occurred on the last play of the game. The record kick was only achieved when the Lions allowed a 36-yard pass play, on FOURTH and NINETEEN. Without this blown play by Detroit, Tucker would not have even been able to attempt his history-making kick. The final score of the game? 19–17. The final score of the Tom Dempsey game, in 1970? 19–17. Two record-setting kicks, both claiming the Lions as the victim, with the exact same score, and both as time expired. And mankind wonders why I am haunted? They can't JUST set a dubious record, with their on-field failures. There has to be an avalanche of epic events, that lead directly to the forgettable outcome.

The venue where the two previously mentioned horrible injuries occurred was the Pontiac Silverdome. It was the home of the Lions from 1975 until 2001. They compiled an overall record of 179–238, with one tie, while playing there. A winning percentage of just under 43%. It was a dreadful, dark, and gloomy place, with a fiberglass roof, and cement circling the entire bowl. The playing surface was basically commercial carpet, placed over more cement, which undoubtably contributed to the injuries that happened there.

Unlike Ford Field, which is in downtown Detroit, the Silverdome was located in middle-of-nowhere Pontiac, where there was literally nothing to do, and nowhere to go, for any pregame activities. Located at the intersection of two major freeways, it was also a nightmare to get out after a game, if you opted to park in the vast lot next to the stadium. I would typically park in a business complex on Featherstone Road, and walk about half a mile.

My weekly ritual? I placed myself in line with hundreds of others, to sample the fare at an Arby's that was on the way to the stadium. Further down the other main street, which was Opdyke Road, there was an establishment or two that could be frequented for a pregame meal, and for libations. But businesses were few and far between, and they were quite a walking distance for those who were not in the best of shape. Overall, not a very fulfilling game day experience.

What was unique, however, were my seats at the venue, which I routinely purchased from an older gentleman. He had season tickets, but he was physically unable to venture out for any games. The seats were in the front row, in the end zone, on the very top level. Very steep, overhanging the front of the end zone. When a touchdown was scored on my end of the stadium, I had to stand up to look down and lean over, just to see the player run in.

The Silverdome held a capacity of just over 80,000 people. It was a vast place. And an incredibly loud one, as well. The acoustics were terrible, and the noise simply reverberated off the concrete enclosure that the stadium essentially was. On its very loudest day, Ford Field could never match the clamor that the Silverdome produced. You could not hear yourself think, let alone talk to the person next to you. The playoff win against the Dallas Cowboys, in January of 1992, was the loudest and most sustained noise level that I will ever experience in my life. Much like the Lions' history, there were simply not enough of these magical moments produced in this building.

In early December of 2017, the place was finally imploded. Well... almost. In keeping with the theme of our journey, the first attempt to demolish the Silverdome was a failure. The imprisonment of the "memories" had to hold on for just another 24 hours. It finally came down on the second try, the very next day. Only our Lions. The site is now home to an Amazon fulfillment center. What screams modern Americana more than that?

Chapter 5

Respite and Reflection

LIFE, AND THE WORLD itself, has changed so very much over the decades. The sports landscape, including both football and all other American sports, is no different. I was an avid viewer for most of my years. However, as the rules and regulations of various sports have changed, my patronage has diminished. College sports are no longer for amateurs alone. NIL (Name, Image, Likeness) has changed the collegiate landscape forever. Athletes can now make millions while developing their own brand, shooting commercials, etc. And without question, they certainly should be allowed to. I want to be clear on this. Universities have long made riches using the names and representations of their student athletes. Add to that, the Transfer Portal allows players to jump from one school to the next, without having to sit out a year. Schools who bring in a player now must outbid another school, to maintain the services of the athlete and keep them from leaving after one season. It is simply the collegiate version of free agency.

I have already spent a lifetime watching a team of players who are paid to "perform" yet still yield amateur results. In addition, the NCAA added a year of eligibility due to COVID-19. Under normal circumstances, an athlete would have five years at a school to complete four years of eligibility. The new rule extended that to six years to complete four seasons. I have even seen players receive seven years of being eligible, in some select cases. Add it all up, and what are you left with? Basically, the minor leagues for professional teams.

Gone are the days when the majority of players would stay with their schools for four years, or even three years, for the select few who made it to the professional level in their particular sport. The rivalries created by the participants who stayed for the duration of their collegiate careers made for compelling viewing. A familiarity was developed from seeing the same names and faces for multiple years. Players would come and go, but they were replaced by new ones who stayed, keeping the rivalries intact. Now, players jump from one school to the next, much like taking a subway system to their next destination, before disembarking from the train.

The current landscape for the coaching profession is much the same. Short stints at a school, and then packing their "carry-on bags" for the flight, in the form of players and assistants that they are taking with them to their new job. This is delightful for them and the athletes, in pursuit of a winning program and the inevitable riches that come with that.

However, this business model has dwindled the scope of my viewership. Self-entitlement becomes an issue, as well. You have a kid who has not yet attended his high school prom, and he is fielding multiple lucrative offers from colleges. He takes the millions, and goes to college, where he is an instant star. What about the young man who has played for his university for a couple of years, has been loyal, yet receives no such reward—at least not in the form of dollars? It is not unreasonable to assume that the player who had everything given to him will expect the same outcome. It's a poor dynamic.

The NBA is a horrible product, in my humble estimation. Virtually zero defense played, poor shooting, entirely too many three-point shots taken, and very few players who possess a mid-range arsenal to complement their game. But without question, they can certainly find creative ways to dunk a basketball. Especially Mac McClung, who—at the NBA festivities in 2023 and 2024— won the slam dunk competition, even though he does not reside on a team roster, as of summer 2024.

Star players dictate where they want to dawdle, essentially stealing the decisions from the general managers, as to which players they want to create their "super teams." If they do not get their way, their pouting and dissatisfaction is carried out in public, until and unless matters are resolved in their favor. While all professional teams have their malcontents, the issue seems to be more prevalent in the particular sport of basketball.

Aside from that, there is also the absurd "load management" factor: this is simply a player taking a night off, when in fact they are able to play and are not injured, have no personal matters pending, etc. I can imagine how some parents must feel, when they spend their hard-earned money to take their child to see a specific player perform, only to find out that the guy they came to see, has made the decision not to play only hours before the game. In addition, the NBA games are often advertised all week on television as "Star player vs. Star player" and not "Team vs. Team," which I think defeats the entire point of the concept of sports as collaborative efforts. Just ridiculous.

To J.J. Redick, the new "coach" of the Los Angeles Lakers: *I hope you are enjoying the actual coach of the team, who also moonlights as the league commissioner. That would be one Lebron James.*

What about MLB? Batting averages have been on a fairly steep decline for years now. Currently, the league-wide average is around 0.236, in June of 2024. Another adverse trend is that strikeouts by hitters are on the rise. They can barely even put the ball in play. Fielding and fundamentals are optional only: outfielders who miss cutoff throws back into the infield, bunting not being utilized situationally, etc. Yes, very riveting.

Pitching? I was fortunate enough to grow up watching the best of the best. Nolan Ryan, the strikeout king, with the all-time record of 5,714 strikeouts. A powerful, fierce competitor, who overpowered hitters. He had 61 shutouts. He also had seven career no-hitters, which also remains an all-time record. Tom Seaver was another excellent pitcher who threw 231 COMPLETE games, with a career-earned run average of 2.86. Far fewer hits given up than innings pitched. He also had 61 shutouts, and one no-hitter. The first two examples were right handers. Here is a great left hander: Steve Carlton. He had 329 wins, the eleventh all-time best. 4,136 strikeouts, the fourth all-time best. 254 career complete games. The list could go on and on. These pitchers, and many unmentioned others, were true workhorses, who not only threw countless innings, but dominated batters while doing so.

In the modern age of baseball, the workloads for pitchers are drastically different. If a starter throws six strong innings, it qualifies as a "quality start." Laughable. Managers have them on a "pitch count" as to not place too much stress and strain on their arms. The worst example of devaluing player performance goes something like this: the rookie standout pitcher for the Pittsburgh Pirates, Paul Skenes, was throwing a no-hitter through seven innings, on July 11th, 2024. I emphasize the date, because it could have been historic.

Instead of giving the young man the chance to achieve something special, the Pirates manager pulled him from the game, after finishing the seventh inning. He claimed that the pitch count (99) had nothing to do with his decision. It was about trusting his own eyes and the player.[2] I know that if I were watching the game, my eyes would have told me that Skenes had my complete trust, while he was dominating a first-place Milwaukee team while only throwing six pitches in his final inning. I wonder how many of the fans in attendance felt swindled out of a chance to say that they witnessed greatness.

Speaking of eyes, here is another example as to why there are less and less of them on the sport. "Specialists" are brought in to sling in the final three innings of the game. This means that teams get to bring in a different pitcher for the end of the game, and often, multiple new pitchers are brought in for a single inning. For example, a left-handed pitcher would be brought in to face a left-handed batter, and vice versa, for just a single out. Very tedious. The aforementioned Hall of Famers, and many like them, just took the ball and got the hitters out. End of story.

To cheapen the sport further, from 2003–2016, the home field in the World Series was given to the league (AL or NL) that won the All-Star Game. Meaning, a team with a much better record during the 162-game regular season would not have home field advantage in the Fall Classic. And it happened multiple times. MLB, in all of their wisdom, decided to place something that important on the outcome of an exhibition game. Just brilliant. Thank goodness they had enough common sense to change it, back in 2017. Then, of course, they cheapened the game again, by implementing the "ghost runner" rule during the shortened COVID season. This rule allows a runner to occupy second base to begin any extra inning, without having to earn it at the plate. This was done to speed up the outcome of games. When the pitch clock rule was put in place in 2023, this accomplished the desired outcome of making the games faster. I will always be of the opinion that the ghost runner rule should have been dropped at that time. Baseball is a sport that has been declining in popularity for years.

Yes, sports have changed dramatically, and not for the better. They are now infused heavily with politics. Slogans adorn uniforms and helmets. The opinion of any person is as valuable as that of any other. However, be that as it may, politics and sports do not need to merge on a television screen, where many people are simply trying to enjoy a well-played sporting contest that isn't inherently political. I have my own opinions, but I would never use any platform to squash the mind of another, into thinking that my way is the only way. The actual politicians? They simply point fingers at one another and take zero responsibility for the sad state of our country. Of course, not all of them behave this way. But more than enough do, which ensures nothing tangible gets done.

The NFL is not devoid of radical changes in its game day presentation either, to be sure. Since 2011, the kickoff was made largely insignificant, when its placement was moved from the 30-yard line to the 35-yard line. It is very boring to watch a kicker blast the ball out of the back of the end zone, which is what happens most of the time. Thankfully, the league has come up with a hybrid kickoff rule, beginning in 2024, that hopefully allows more returns.

Additionally, penalties for hitting the quarterback are absurd. How you can you expect a defender—who is contorting his body, being pushed and leaned on by a 300-pound offensive lineman, and with a full head of steam—to only contact the quarterback in a specific part of the body, and in a certain way? It is not feasible. Why not just make the game a flag football contest? It seems to be well on its way already. Horrible officiating. Flags thrown, and then picked up, with the resolution being that "there was no foul on the play." Then why throw it in the first place? Reviewing plays frame by frame, with new technology at the touch of a fingertip, and still leaving doubt as to whether the correct call was made, have long been a trend. Indecision, miscommunication, and chaos. Whether or not I am watching the Lions, I do not want to see the outcome of a game decided by a bogus call. Or a non-call. Ask New Orleans Saints fans about the 2018 NFC Championship Game. Easily the most blatant missed call that I have ever witnessed in my sports-watching life, which cost a fanbase and a franchise a trip to the Super Bowl. The integrity of the league took a hit on that day.

Player safety? The reason given by the league for moving the kickoff spot was to "avoid the high-speed collisions" that occurred on those plays. How compassionate of them. Then, the league expanded the schedule from 16 games to 17 in 2021, adding more wear and tear to the players, who risk serious injury (or their lives) while playing the game. Teams have to play on traditional Sundays, and then turn around, on a very short week, and do it again on Thursdays. But of course, with the "best interest" of the union in mind. Please, just stop.

And now, the league is in talks with the representatives of the players, making every effort to extend the regular season to 18 games. As a fan, I would love to watch another game. But I understand that players are having an aversion to this groundswell, and for good reason. In the end, it IS about money. Just leave it at that, and don't pretend to care about the well-being of the athletes. At least 10 former players have filed a class action lawsuit against the league, professing that their claims for healthcare, which were collectively bargained for, were denied. If proven to be true, this is certainly unscrupulous.

Gambling? While in Las Vegas during the 2024 Super Bowl week, members of the Kansas City Chiefs and San Francisco 49ers, as well as their coaches and staff members, were disallowed from partaking in gambling, of ANY kind. No cards, slots, nothing. Betting on the sport that they play is obviously forbidden. But being barred from walking into a casino, with family members and friends, and rolling the dice? It seems that the Powers That Be wanted the teams to take an "all business" approach towards the game. Of course, while the NFL has long partnered with the sports betting agencies, making obscene amounts of money. And while playing the Super Bowl in one of the most notorious betting capitals in the world.

Quite a split screen that would entail: on one side, an entity raking in fortunes from wagering, solely because of the players who perform. On the other side, the same entity warning said players, with a wagging finger, to do nothing of the sort. Complete hypocrisy. My flame continues to burn out…When I need an accelerant, I still turn to the NFL, and inherently, the Lions. I no longer watch for 10 straight hours, to view all the time-slotted games, because of the transformation that the league continues to go through.

No, I am not an old man shouting, "Get off of my lawn!" I understand and realize that change is imminent. I simply do not agree that all of it is for the better, or even necessary. If all the transition is so wonderful, then why is our world such a mess? Why are sports largely about personalities, and less about the games themselves? Some traditions, in sports and otherwise, are just better left unchanged. Simplicity... These days, I merely catch the scores and highlights later at night, given from the standpoint of the best in the business, Scott Van Pelt. A single moment of the home team, however, will never go unnoticed. Possibly witnessing a new and inventive way to lose, even in the midst of a rare winning season, is simply too salacious to pass by.

I never chose the Lions. Rather, they are much like the cat that appears on your doorstep, that you feed and nurture out of the kindness of your heart. Yes, my family cared for such an animal, until he departed, having happily satisfied his palate. The other "feline" that I have been confronted with has never left me. I doubt it ever will...

Chapter 6

Getting It Wrong

CUE UP THE MIDWAY music. Watching the Lions for a lifetime has truly been sideshow carnival entertainment. We have touched on some of their on-field "performance." That is merely one side of the coin, with their off-field lunacy being the other; however, until the 2023-2024 season, the coin has always spelled failure, regardless of which side showed itself face-up when flipped.

Allow me to begin this chapter of off-field failures with my all-time favorite incident. In August of 2007, defensive line coach Joe Cullen cruised through a Wendy's drive through, late at night. Innocent enough. The obstacle (or lack thereof) however, was clothing. Mr. Cullen rolled through completely naked, devoid of a single garment. Which made me wonder—at any point when his night of drinking began, was he coherent enough to realize that he had no attire on? Perhaps it was removed during the binge? Yet, he was still in control enough to navigate a motor vehicle into a winding drive through and place an order? Which, according to the store employees, was a single burger combo. Mission accomplished! It is only fair to mention that he has since turned his life around, was contrite publicly, and remains employed as a coach in the league.[3]

Cullen was not fired by Rod Marinelli, the Lions' head coach at the time. Instead, he was sent to an alcohol rehab program,[4] and he remained a part of the team until Marinelli was dismissed after the 2008 winless season. The team was in the midst of a very good season in 2007, with a 6–2 record at the halfway point. At a team Halloween party, quarterback Jon Kitna donned a costume[5] resembling a naked man, and his wife decorated herself as a Wendy's drive through employee.

While the media and the public made light of the personal difficulties that Cullen was enduring, the episode caused quite the controversy. It also brought a distraction to the team, when it finally hit the local media and reporters asked Kitna about why he chose to do it. At first, the Wendy's incident was not picked up by the media. I can say so unequivocally, because it happened in August, and the season then entered late October without a whisper about it in the local news. One week after the Wendy's caper, Cullen again was pulled over, and again he was found to be driving intoxicated. The event did NOT go unnoticed twice, and the first arrest came to light soon thereafter. Still, as mentioned, the team WAS having success, which only became unraveled after the Halloween party.[6] It presented quite the furor. The "Lions only" correlation? Although they did win the game AFTER the costume fiasco six days later in a 44–7 thrashing of Denver, they then proceeded to lose six consecutive games, dropping their record to 6–8, and once again failed to qualify for the playoffs.

The momentum of the now very public Wendy's incident, and the Kitna costume mockery of Cullen, became a national story. Cullen and the Lions were a laughingstock again. From 6–2, to 6–8, after the story blew up. Coincidence? No, I tend to think not.

I mean, damn, how much of their history can be attributed to happenstance? The next season was the winless 2008 campaign. As we recall, in 1958, when leaving the franchise, Bobby Layne famously and allegedly uttered that the team "will not win for 50 years." Well, almost exactly 50 years to the day, the Lions went winless for the ENTIRE season. Perhaps he meant to change just one word, from "FOR 50 years" to "IN 50 years."

The following examples are in no way meant to be humorous. They depict loss of life, and, to be concise, devastation. With the seventh overall pick of the 1987 draft, the team selected defensive lineman Reggie Rogers. In his rookie year, he played in only six games. His absence was reported to be the result of attending treatment for emotional counseling, which was rumored to also include sessions for chemical and alcohol dependency. Which, with his known public record, seems plausible.

On October 20th, 1988, his vehicle struck another, and three people were killed. He was found to have a blood-alcohol content well over the legal limit in Michigan. In 1990, he was convicted of vehicular homicide, and he spent 13 months in prison. After short stints with other teams, he played in a total of 15 games during his career. Rogers was found deceased in his home in Seattle, in October of 2013. The autopsy revealed his passing was caused by a combination of cocaine and ethanol intoxication.[7]

In the second round of the 2011 draft, the Lions selected wide receiver Titus Young, out of Boise State. His troubles began well before making the pro roster. In college, his coach suspended him for violating team rules, initially for three games. The suspension was soon made indefinite. He did not return to the field during that season, which was in 2008. Despite his immense talent, he was passed over in the draft, until Detroit took him. During his time with the Lions, he displayed more disciplinary issues, including a verbal confrontation with one of his coaches. This incident occurred on November 18th of 2012. It was the last game he would play in the league. He was deactivated for the next two games, and placed on injured reserve on December fourth, ending his season, and playing career. Twenty-six total games. He also sucker-punched one of his teammates during his time with the Lions.[8]

In February of 2013, he was claimed from the waiver wire by the St. Louis Rams, one day after the Lions permanently released him. Only 10 days later, the Rams released him, with the team stating that they wanted to change course.[9] You can draw your own conclusions.

Soon thereafter, his legal problems began to emerge. In early May of 2013, he was arrested twice on the same day: once for suspected drunk driving, and again for trying to steal his impounded vehicle from a tow yard. In August of 2013, he acquired burglary charges, and a bench warrant was issued after he missed his court hearing for these allegations. In December of the same year, his trial was again delayed while he was in the hospital for an undisclosed treatment.[10]

Sadly, the violent nature of his alleged crimes only escalated as time went on. He was arrested in July of 2014 on five counts of battery, for punching and attacking his then attorney. For this charge, he received five years' probation, and one year of inpatient treatment at a California rehab center. In late January of 2016, Young was again arrested for assault with a deadly weapon, and for felony battery. He received a four-year sentence in April of 2017, and he was released in December of 2018.[11]

Well-documented mental illnesses long plagued him. He was diagnosed with bipolar disorder in 2013. Add that to the many legal charges, and it was quite an infamous year for Mr. Young. It just happened to be the EXACT year that Reggie Rogers was found dead. I always ask myself, how many grave misfortunes can be brushed off as minor coincidences, regarding a singular franchise? Perhaps you are beginning to wonder the same?

Finally, after one misfire, the Lions made another attempt to foray into "Mr. Rogers' Neighborhood." With the second overall pick in the 2003 draft, the team selected wide receiver Charles Rogers[12] out of Saginaw, Michigan, from Michigan State University. A hometown kid makes it big in the NFL. It was a great story, at least initially.

Twice, while in college, he tested positive for marijuana. Yes, I know it is now legal in Michigan. However, in the early 2000s, it was not. This finding should have served as a major red flag to the Lions, when considering to spend such a high draft pick. Predictably, though, the team ignored the warning signs and chose him nonetheless.

His resume is as follows: five games into his rookie season, he broke his clavicle and missed the rest of the season. In the first game of the 2004 season, he once again suffered the exact same injury, this time causing him to miss the entire season.

During recovery from these injuries, Rogers became addicted to Vicodin. He violated the substance policy of the NFL multiple times, leading to a four-game suspension in 2005. The Lions attempted to recoup bonus money that they had paid him, claiming he violated a clause in his contract. He did not repay the money, and the team filed a lawsuit against him. It was a complete mess.

Much like the other previously highlighted examples, his legal troubles began fairly soon after his extraction from the league in 2008, when he was charged with assault and battery on his girl-friend. Those charges were dropped. In March of 2009, he was jailed for probation violation. And later that year, he was again arrested when found passed out behind the wheel of his car.[13] There were other violations soon afterwards, but I think you get the point. Just very sad...

In a 2009 interview with ESPN,[14] he admitted that his downfall was due to his lifestyle. His career statistics? He played in 15 total games, with 36 receptions and four touchdowns. And in November of 2019, he passed away, at age 38, from his battle with liver cancer.

There were wasted resources by the team throughout the years, to be certain. But these stories of human lives being destroyed off-field are far more disheartening. The list of on-field only busts is lengthy, with far too many to mention. QB Chuck Long (1986), WR Mike Williams (2005), QB Andre Ware (1990), and QB Joey Harrington (2002) were all first-round choices, who all fell far short of expectations. Thankfully, these men did NOT wreak havoc on society or themselves, nor did they place the franchise in embarrassing situations.

Say it with me: "Only the Lions."

Chapter 7

Coaches

NOT A STELLAR LIST. Detroit has been a graveyard for coaches. No gentleman mentioned here was ever able to land another head coaching job in the league. Think of each heading, with their names and years of service, as headstones. In the Motor City, we like to describe their failures as being "Lionized."

The shell-shocked looks on these coaches' faces, their public frustrations, and their memorable quotes are indelible. They were mostly likable men, who were simply not equipped to be head coaches. Overmatched and out-maneuvered. Exacerbating the situation of each was being given the opportunity by an organization and management that had failed at every turn, in every way, for a lifetime of most who have watched them. It's not as if the Lions have not tried. They certainly have. The results simply were not there.

Let me begin where my recollection starts.

Monte Clark (1978–1984)

A record of 43-63-1. Two playoff appearances, one of which was the "prayer" game. It certainly was not his fault that Eddie Murray missed the kick. Invariably, it simply equated to watching the same movie, repeatedly. You are well aware of how it will end. That fateful New Year's Eve just happened to be my initial viewing of the film. I was saddened for him on that day, and I often remember the moment. He passed away in September of 2009.

Darryl Rogers (1985–1988)

An unmitigated disaster. No playoff appearances. After yet another loss, he uttered: "What does a coach have to do to around here to get fired?"[15]

Perhaps the answer to that question is a career record of 18–40. An interesting tidbit: In 1985, the team accrued a record of 7–9, which was by far his best as head coach. In four of the seven wins, the Lions beat a team that made the playoffs that year. A statistic such as this, veiled by the constant clown show, is a perfect example of what has long been defined by the organization as "success." He didn't have a bad first year; however, it was just a tumble off a cliff from there. He passed away in July of 2018.

Wayne Fontes (1988–1996)

Yes! Good ole Wayno. Affable, approachable. As mentioned, Wayne Fontes is the Lions' all-time leader in wins, forever remembered for being the sideline leader in the blowout victory over Dallas in January of 1992. Four playoff appearances, and two division titles. The division title, which he guided the team to in 1993, was their last, until they broke through in 2023. It had been 30 years... wow. Three straight playoff showings from 1993–1995. This run also accounted for the best stretch the team has ever accrued, since having four straight winning seasons from 1969–1972.

Regrettably, Chuck Hughes died on the field in 1971. So, in a strange way, the brief success that Fontes enjoyed during his tenure is also tied to one of the saddest moments in professional sports. In the midst of good, bad firmly implants itself, in remembrance, and in any current moment. Only the Lions.

Fontes' numbers speak for themselves. Overall, he was a winner, agreed? Ummm… no. His regular season coaching record was 66–67, and 1–4 in the playoffs, for a dossier of 67–71. Not to be forgotten, he was also blessed with having Barry Sanders on his roster, for all of his Lions coaching years (minus 1988, but I couldn't care less). Thank you, Mr. Fontes, for being largely responsible for providing the best football day of my life, up until then. Did I say "up until then?" Hmmm, perhaps there are blue skies ahead. Not in this chapter, however…

Bobby Ross (1997–2000)

The disciplinarian. Authoritative. Arrived to the organization after five seasons with the San Diego Chargers, which included two division titles, three playoff trips, and their first Super Bowl appearance. An overall record of 47–33. Finally, a stern coach, who would provide the focus and toughness that was lacking in the Wayne Fontes era. Easily upset, Ross often showed his emotions publicly, and was known for tirades in front of reporters. He also came up with creative outbursts that left fans trying to decipher what he meant, such as, "WHOMP WHOMP WHOMP, abandon ship!"[16] Perhaps he was feeling that his players were giving up in a game? I remain miffed about that one! Still, it was must-see television. He wore his heart on his sleeve, to be sure.

One game in particular stood out. In November of 1999, the Lions played Arizona. With just over five minutes left in the game, defensive back Terry Fair scooped up a fumble and returned it 35 yards for a touchdown, cutting the Arizona lead to 23–19. Perfect. Kick the extra point, cut the lead to three, get the ball back, and tie or win the game. Instead, Ross elected to go for two points, which of course failed, leaving the score at 23–19. Always dramatic when losing, the Lions certainly DID get the ball back, and they drove deep into Arizona's chip shot field goal territory.

Because of the earlier decision to go for two points, and still down by four, Detroit was forced to attempt a pass on fourth down. Is anyone waiting with bated breath as to the outcome of the play?

After the game, when asked about the decision to go for two points, Ross mentioned having a card, which lists what decision should be made in specific situations. What card was that, Bobby? The joker? You felt as though you should take a risk that day? The only thing you risked that afternoon was… winning. Finally, he threatened to give "bus tickets out of town"[17] to players who failed to fall in line. He did not follow through with that threat. Greyhound Bus revenue took a decided downturn during his tenure, I would imagine. On November 5th, 2000, the Lions lost at home to Miami. In the televised press conference following the game, Ross suggested that he had failed, and that the team should have been a model of himself. He was somber, to be sure.

However, nobody could predict what was to transpire next. The very next day, midseason, he resigned as head coach. The Lions were 5–4, tied for second place, and NOT in the midst of a hopeless season. Lions Assistant Coach and former Michigan Head Coach, Gary Moeller, finished the season with a record of 4–3.

Ross compiled a record of 27–30, with two playoff losses, as coach of the team. The scrutiny was simply too intense for him. Mr. Ross, you have been "Lionized!"

Marty Mornhinweg (2001–2002)

The list couldn't get worse, could it? Marty Mornhinweg has a record of 5–27 in his two seasons. But the dismal record is not what Marty remains famous for. Oh, I almost forgot to mention, his overall winning percentage (0.156) is the worst of any head coach the team has ever had, except for a guy named Bull Karcis, who lost all eight games that he coached in 1942.

In late November of 2002, Mornhinweg made one of the most myopic decisions in league history. In the early 2000s, overtime was sudden death. This rule was changed in 2010, allowing each team a possession, provided that a touchdown was not scored on the initial drive. Instead of doing what any and every coach would do after winning the coin toss, Mornhinweg made the irreconcilable choice to give the ball to the Chicago Bears. It was especially windy that day, and Mornhinweg thought that he could use the wind to the Lions' advantage by making the other team have to fight through it. Yes, he famously "took the wind."[18] Right on cue, after being given the ball, the Bears drove down the field, and kicker Paul Edinger made a 40-yard game winner. Hey Marty… with the rules being what they were on that day, it would not have mattered if an epic monsoon had taken place. You always, always… take the ball.

The outcome was not the only hilarity. The Lions blew a 10-point lead in the final three minutes of the same game. On fourth down and 20, with under a minute to play in regulation, an obviously injured Jim Miller, the Bears' QB, rolled out and fell to the ground.

With the entire Lions defense unable to place a hand on him to end the play, Miller got back into his wheelchair, pushed on the rims to propel himself, and completed a 33-yard pass downfield, which put his team in position to kick the field goal, which sent the game to overtime.

On the game-winning drive in the extra session, the Bears faced a third and 18. They picked up 15 yards on the play. With the ball resting on the Detroit 30, the Bears opted to pass on a long field goal, given the windy conditions. Instead, they ran a play on fourth down, picking up the necessary yardage to continue the drive. That… is what is known as a smart coaching decision, Mr. Mornhinweg.

From there, the Bears maneuvered into better kicking range, and we all know the rest. His retort when asked about the decision? He said that the people who had attended the game were well-informed and as a result knew that it was the correct call, then and now, and that it would still be correct 10 years later. No, Marty, it certainly was NOT the right call. However, there IS good news. Your complete lack of foresight will always have you firmly placed in NFL annals. Your reasoning and belief that you made the right choice? That firmly places you in the "anal" realm. But I really enjoyed when you rode off on your motorcycle during training camp, ending practice and "sending a message." To be certain, they are wonderful machines. I hope that you caught a good wind that afternoon.

Steve Mariucci (2003–2005)

The savior. The one who would rescue the Lions. He arrived from a great franchise, the San Francisco 49ers, with an impressive track record. A 60–43 overall record, which included four playoff appearances, and three post season victories. He certainly had me fooled. I was more excited about his hiring than any other coach. Like all of the others, he was never a head coach again.

At the time of his signing, the Lions gave him the largest contract for a coach in league history. He compiled a record of 15–28, and then he was fired with five games left to play in the 2005 season. His replacement to finish that season, on an interim basis? None other than Dick Jauron, who was the head coach of the Bears in the "take the wind" game! How fun it is to connect dots! Always some bizarre correlation, directly attached to my team and their sad history. I enjoyed watching Mariucci when his eyes would bug out of their sockets, after yet another Joey Harrington miscue!

Thank you, sir, for the Mariucci Family Foundation, which helps underprivileged young people and their families. This says everything about your true character. I remember what it was like to grow up with little, if anything. But yes, you were also victimized by the twilight zone that is becoming a head coach in the Motor City.

Rod Marinelli (2006-2008)

Actually, I really liked the work ethic that this guy brought. He was a great defensive line coach. Hard-nosed, and a tireless worker. During his 10 years with Tampa Bay, the Bucs recorded more sacks than any team in the league. In his first two seasons with the Lions, the team won a total of 10 games. In his career as the Detroit head coach, also just 10 victories. Wait… what did I miss? He was the coach for three years, not just two. Oh, yes. Now I remember. As we are fully aware, the Lions were the first team to go winless in a sixteen-game season. And history tells us that Mr. Marinelli was the head coach of that unit, in 2008. It must have been horrific to be a coach or player on that squad. As a fan, I will never forget. The butt of jokes by late night talk show hosts, and the center of negativity by television analysts, on virtually every network. Just an utter catastrophe. Undoubtably, the lowest point that the franchise has ever reached. His character, however, was never a question.

Thank you, Rod, for your service to our country, in the Vietnam War. And yes, for your time with the Lions, as well. It couldn't have been easy.

Jim Schwartz (2009–2013)

He was hired away from the Tennessee Titans, where he served as their defensive coordinator. And a very good one, before and after his tenure with Detroit. After an initial two-win season in 2009, the team steadily improved, and they reached the playoffs in 2011 with a record of 10–6.

The Monday night game that season against the Bears was by far the loudest I have ever heard at Ford Field. An electrifying 88-yard run by Jahvid Best blew the roof off the place. The crowd was responsible for the Chicago offense committing nine false starts. Nine? Wow. I am not aware of that many in any other game throughout league history, but it certainly is the most since that October evening in 2011.

Six days later, the San Francisco 49ers came to Ford Field and ruined the Lions unblemished record. During the post-game handshake between coaches, 49ers coach Jim Harbaugh slapped Schwartz on the back, not stopping to say a word. Schwartz, obviously upset, went after Harbaugh, and a skirmish between the teams began, extending to the tunnel. It was hilarious.

After the 5–0 start to the season, Detroit finished the remaining 11 games 5–6, but they still managed to qualify for the playoffs as a wild card team, where they lost in the first round to New Orleans. From there, the team went 4–12 in 2012, and 7–9 in 2013. He was fired after that season. Overall, a listless record of 29–51, with the one playoff berth.

Jahvid Best is worth mentioning again. An explosive dual threat running back, he was great at catching the ball out of the backfield. Since Barry Sanders gave the organization the proverbial middle finger, the Lions went through many running backs, while never finding anyone close to his talents. Barry stands alone. Unfortunately, Best had a history of suffering concussions. He had another such occurrence, in the San Francisco game, which turned out to be his last ever played in the league. After his loss, the team was left without a suitable backup, and they relied heavily on their passing game, making them predictable to opposing defenses. They were among the best in passing statistics, and at the bottom in rushing, because of the lack of running attempts. As we remember, numbers sometimes lie!

Strangely enough, the team seemed to be ascending under Schwartz, until the handshake fiasco. Am I suggesting that incident alone was the cause of Schwartz's failings? Of course not. That would be a stretch. We are, however, referencing the history of the Lions. Success goes askew for the most seemingly hairsplitting of circumstances. And on the same day, within three hours, he lost a vital cog in the offense in Jahvid Best, and then his mind, when he went after Harbaugh. And after losing to the 49ers, they were never the same team under his guidance. There is no questioning that.

His greatest moment as a coach at Ford Field was unsurprisingly not AS the Lions coach, but against them. Returning in 2014, after his firing, as the defensive coordinator with Buffalo, Schwartz allowed his players to carry him off the field after defeating the Lions. Congratulations, Jim. You reached the "mountaintop" of the coaching profession. Quite an ascent… from the ground to the shoulders of your players.

I do recall that Schwartz was quite the rock-and-roll music fan. A classic rock connotation does not apply in this instance, however. With regard to his time as head coach, more apropos would be the Four Tops' Motown classic hit, "It's The Same Old Song."[19] Lionized!

Jim Caldwell (2014-2017)

As a rookie head coach with the Indianapolis Colts in 2009, Jim Caldwell took his team to the Super Bowl. He was the second first-year coach to accomplish the feat, since George Seifert won the big game in the 1989 season, defeating the San Diego Chargers. The losing coach in that game? The aforementioned Bobby Ross.

Players would run through a wall for Caldwell. They respected him, and vice versa. Cerebral, he was, and never showed much emotion. With the Lions, he had three winning seasons, and two playoff appearances in four years. Both were losses, of course, completing the Lions' record-setting, consecutive playoff loss streak. On Monday through Saturday, he may well have been a great motivator. But on Sundays, he often took on the role of a deer in headlights. Many times during his tenure, the team looked unprepared and caught off guard. His questionable usage of the clock and time outs, and his unwillingness to throw a challenge flag, left his skills as a tactician in question. Still, his is a great record for any Lions head coach, especially compared to the others on this list.

So why let him go, you may be wondering? After two consecutive 9–7 seasons, in 2016 and 2017, second year General Manager Bob Quinn fired Caldwell. His reason why? A 9–7 record did not come close to meeting the team's goals. Interesting, considering that while he was the GM of the team, the record shows that he was 31–43, with one tie, for a lamentable percentage of 0.420. Conversely, as coach of the Lions, Caldwell had a winning percentage of 0.545. You would have to go back to Joe Schimdt (1967–1972) to find a Lions head coach with a better percentage. And just barely at 0.547. It was you, Mr. Quinn, who was "not nearly good enough" even by Lions standards. Caldwell was 36–30 as head coach in the Motor City, and his overall career slate stands at 62–50. A good football man, who is widely respected throughout the league.

There are two other coaches that will be mentioned, both past and present, in the following chapters. One who deserves much credit, and the other who was so bad that he requires further refocusing of myself, just to put it into proper perspective. Reliving this list of failures, has truly exhausted me. It is past due time for some good vibes. I am titillated to move along. One of my favorite songs is named "The Best of Times"[20] by the classic rock band Styx. Let us relive all of these such moments, in our next entry.

Chapter 8
The Best of Times

No content available.

(This chapter is intentionally left blank.)

Chapter 9

Just Kidding!

MUSIC IS A WONDERFUL elixir for the soul. It invokes memories of loved ones, of a certain time at a certain place, or simply of lyrics that remind oneself of cherished moments; these are all examples of how these melodies exemplify the lives that we maintain, and our past that we remember. The Lions, ironically, made one such contribution to my upbringing, with a tune all their own. Well, remotely, at best. Several players recorded a parody of the Queen song, "Another One Bites the Dust"[21] and it hit Detroit's radio airwaves in September of 1980. Lions defensive back Jimmy "Spiderman" Allen penned the lyrics for this musical parody that I found effing hilarious.[22] The rap-infused tune depicted the team's early season success. If you are unfamiliar, please Google the lyrics.

At the time, I was an impressionable 15-year-old who had recently adopted the Beatles as his musical idols, and the track was an awakening. People were dancing in the streets, and the energy was infectious.

The team began the season with a record of 4–0, led by rookie running back Billy Sims. After the fast start, the Lions lost seven of their last 10, finishing 9–7, and, of course, missing the play-offs. Ex-Lion Doug English, a member of the 1980 team, publicly despised the song,[23] suggesting that it was the reason for the down-fall of the team. For me, it changed everything. It is not hyperbole to say so, because of the excitement surrounding the brief success that the team had, and the raucous reaction to the song. This was the time in my life when the Lions seeped into my soul forever. In the previous seven seasons before 1980, they had done nothing. I was a pre-teen, learning about the world. And although I knew what the results were, year by year, and week by week, I merely hoped that they would win to spite my father.

September of 1980 is when I actually began to watch fully, and I became emotionally invested. Jimmy Allen passed away in December of 2019. He was a two-time Super Bowl champion, while a member of the Pittsburgh Steelers. Rest in peace, "Spiderman." Because of your iconic voice and lyrics, our team was the epicenter of the league, if only for a month. I needed it, and you were the driving force in delivering that. You are forever one of my all-time favorite Lions.

The most exciting player that I have ever watched (and ever will) is Barry Sanders. What he did on a football field is forever etched into league highlights history. I could explain what was wit-nessed by many, but words alone would never do it any justice. If by chance you are unfamiliar, simply look up some of his clips. It is truly mind boggling. He was set to become the all-time leading rusher in league history, when he abruptly retired from the league after the 1998 season. He famously sent a fax to a newspaper in Wichita, Kansas, to announce his retirement. No cameras, news-papers, etc. Just a nondescript gesture, as is his nature. Humble, quiet, never drawing any attention to himself. Just very classy. The documentary named "Bye Bye Barry" provides more insight as to his decision to leave the game, which was primarily due to the lack of team success and frustration with team management.

In the NFL of today, players routinely carry out scripted celebrations after scoring a touchdown. My favorite memory of Mr. Sanders? After yet again embarrassing a defender on his way to the end zone, he simply handed the ball to the official. No dances, no mockery of the opposing team. Again, nothing but class. A Hall of Famer.

There were some contentious times following his retirement. It was because of a lawsuit regarding a portion of his signing bonus, which the Lions wanted returned, because Sanders had not fulfilled his contract when he retired. Sanders and his agent asked the team for his release, in exchange for paying back the total amount owed to the team. This agreement would allow him to continue his career with another team. The Lions refused to grant him the release. This was petty, and it was the wrong decision from the team. The team was lousy, on and off the field, and Sanders had been through enough. He never played again, and he was only 1,457 yards short of the rushing record, then held by Walter Payton, and now belonging to Emmitt Smith. With more than enough football left in him, Sanders would have shattered the record.

He brought joy and excitement to our fanbase, with his one-of-a-kind running style. As the face of the franchise, his humility and sophistication garnered respect throughout the league. Fences were mended between him and the team over time, and he finally returned to the team as an ambassador in 2017. He remains a fixture, with regular appearances at games, and in public. His statue, which was long overdue to be created and unveiled, rests outside of Ford Field. He meant everything to the team and city during his playing days. Thank goodness that management got it right in this instance and welcomed him back. He will always be the greatest Lion of all time.

December 31st of 1983 was when I had my first premonition, as to what would become my life as a Lions fan. In 1983, the Lions won the division title. Life was great. The team was beginning to have success. I legally became a "man" that year. Rest assured, Alice Cooper... I was 18, and I liked it! Their playoff game was against the San Francisco 49ers. Despite being a decided underdog, the Lions kept the game close throughout, despite an incredible five interceptions by Lions QB Gary Danielson.

With just under five minutes left in the contest, Billy Sims ran for a short touchdown, and after the extra point, the Lions led 23-17. Chaos ensued within the group I was watching with. This WAS the moment of vindication that I had been waiting for. This would be my reward for enduring the humiliation of always defending them. Then, it began... One of the all-time greats, Joe Montana, led his team to a touchdown, hitting Freddie Solomon with just over a minute left. From triumph.... to forlorn.

The ride was just beginning, however. Smartly and efficiently, Danielson led the Lions back down the field. He avoided pressure, and he made accurate throws. The methodical drive left the ball resting on the 26-yard line, with seconds remaining.

Called upon was Eddie Murray, the Lions kicker, who was very reliable for the entire season. He had already made three field goals in this game, one of which was from 54 yards, a league record at that time. This attempt, to virtually win the game, was from 43 yards. My naive mindset? No worries whatsoever. To be concise, premature celebration. Never a wise endeavor when siding with the Lions.

Perhaps having more perception and awareness than I had, was Lions coach Monte Clark. With the camera fixed on him, he provided one of the most unforgettable images in league history. Moments before the kick, he formed his hands in prayer. No matter. The attempt went just wide right, swept away by the subtle bay area winds. A mere five seconds and one kneel down remained.

Thank you, my Lions, for not only ringing in the new year, but my adulthood, as well. Only one other time in my football life was I more despondent, but we have yet to reach that point in our journey. The "best" must be saved for last.

When I first saw my father after the game, he was at the ready, with a wink and a grin. For years, he did everything he could to warn me, short of drawing me a map with the location of the landmine to be sidestepped. Thank you, Michael Bannon, for the useful and wise life lesson.

As previously noted, the playoff game in January of 1992 was an unforgettable experience. January 5th of 1992, for myself, stands alone. Would a Super Bowl appearance be the only event that could supersede that memorable day? In terms of historical significance, the answer is yes. It would be surreal to witness, without question. However, knowing that I would never be able to afford to attend, I may knock it down just a notch. An exhale would be a more accurate illustration, knowing that I lived to watch it, just once.

Aside from Barry Sanders and Calvin Johnson, there have been many great Lions players throughout their history. Those I have watched include Chris Spielman, a warrior at linebacker who embodied the team spirit every year he played. Four pro bowls, and he holds virtually every tackling record for the team. He is currently a member of the Lions front office. Make no mistake, the emergence of the team as contenders has his fingerprint plastered all over it. He is a member of the Lions' ring of honor.

Bubba Baker and Doug English, who anchored the "Silver Rush," which was the name given to the defensive line that harassed quarterbacks like no other unit in Lions history in the late 1970s and early 1980s.

Robert Porcher is the all-time leader in sacks for the team. Kevin Glover was a fantastic center, paving the way for many of the spectacular runs that Barry thrilled us with. He was a three-time pro bowler.

Herman Moore is a legendary receiver for the team. He held many team receiving records, which were only surpassed later by Calvin Johnson. In the playoff win against Dallas, the rookie caught six passes, with one going for a touchdown. He was the first-round pick of the team in 1991. Four pro bowls. A great choice.

Lomas Brown played on the same offensive line with Glover. A superb blocker. Seven straight pro bowl selections. He is also a member of the Lions ring of honor.

Brett Perriman, who played alongside Moore, was another talented receiver.

Billy Sims was a classic running back, whose career was cut short by injuries. In just 60 career games, he amassed more than 5,000 yards, with 42 touchdowns. He was a three-time pro bowler.

There are others, and I apologize to any that I have omitted. The franchise has employed some talented players, and there were many exciting games and moments produced by them. Just not enough winning, paired with losing in unprecedented fashion.

Chapter 10

Not Their Fault

OF COURSE, THE FRANCHISE has shot itself in the foot for eons. As you gain a reputation throughout the league for being a punchline, the officials will follow in kind, in terms of their lack of respect towards you. The Lions have been completely robbed a number of times.

Until September of 2017, I had never been aware of the 10 second runoff rule. In 2017, the Lions began the season with a nice 2–0 start. Trying to make it three straight against Atlanta, here is what transpired. Golden Tate scored a touchdown with eight seconds left in the game, giving the Lions the virtual game clincher. The place was bonkers. Or... did he? Upon review, it was clear that his knee was down before the ball crossed the goal line.

No worries, I quickly told myself. Remain positive. They still have time for one or two plays.

Because the play was initially ruled a touchdown, the clock was stopped, and the play went under review by the replay officials. Coaches are unable to throw the challenge flag with under two minutes remaining. The call was then reversed (correctly). If the correct call of the runner being down was made initially, the play would have continued, the clock would have continued to run, and with the Lions having no time outs remaining, it is possible that time would have run out. But the on-field officials ruled it a touchdown, and the booth above opted to review it.

It is a foolish rule. If the officials decide to stop the clock on their own, then without question, any time remaining should be restored and not taken away. How is that the fault of the Lions? They obviously did not ask for any review. Just another Sunday afternoon of nerve endings being fragmented. What else is new? Some might say that a rule is a rule. To that, I throw my hands up. I cannot say anything to the contrary. But this, I do know: until that day, virtually no person was aware of such an obscure rule. And of course, the Lions had to be the first victim of it.

The referee came out to announce a return to a running clock and that the team had a 10-second runoff. That meant the game was over.

The entire place was stunned and confused. Instead of a 3–0 start, they were 2–1 and missed the playoffs by one game. Quinn fired Caldwell at the end of the season, and the Matt Patricia era was ushered in.

In October of 2015, the Lions played at Seattle. With just under two minutes remaining in the game, Calvin Johnson surged towards the end zone, and while airborne just inside the one-yard line, Seattle defender Cam Chancellor punched the ball out of his hands, before Johnson reached the goal line. The ball bounced around in the end zone, where K.J. Wright intentionally batted the ball out of the back of it. This action, by rule, is illegal. The officials ruled the play a touchback, giving the Seahawks possession of the ball.

This was far from the correct ruling. Wright should have been flagged for illegal batting, giving the Lions the ball at the spot of the fumble, plus half the distance to the goal line. Essentially, Detroit should have given the ball, with a first down inside the one-yard line. Just another horrible application of their own written book, by the NFL. Again, what is even more deplorable, is that when such an instance occurs, not having the purpose or wherewithal to correct it on the spot. The NFL rulebook may well be "black and white" in the definitions of rules. And black and white is what is needed, for the set of crayons that should come with the coloring book that they apply each week. Give me a chance to waste time writing a rule that will not be enforced when a clear example of it presents itself, and I can certainly scribble outside of the lines. Because there certainly seems to be no benefit for playing within them.

Literally, on a weekly basis, we roast marshmallows, waiting while officials go under the hood and attempt to decipher whether or not a receiver made a clean catch. Welcome to the advent of this futile exercise. The sitcom (and venue) starring officials changes each Sunday, but the Lions consistently have been cast, from one episode to the next. In the 2010 season opener against Chicago, everyone's hope for a fast start to the season was halted by the stripes. Calvin Johnson (yes, him again) caught a long touchdown pass from Shaun Hill, who was in the game for an injured Matthew Stafford. Yes, he caught the pass. The play gave the Lions the lead, with only 25 seconds remaining. Always spectacular, Johnson went high above the shorter defender, came down with one foot down, two feet down, knee down, and rear end down, with FULL possession of the ball. That is a touchdown. While rolling over, he braced himself with his left hand. In his right hand was the ball, which squirted out when he placed the hand down. This was loooong after he had established control and possession of the ball.

What color do you want your crayon to be today? The Bears already wear black, yes? I stand corrected. It is actually navy blue. Shall we use their orange accents for disregarding the boundaries, in this particular instance? The officials ruled that Johnson did not have control of the ball throughout the play, which famously began the debate of "completing the process" for what qualifies as a catch. I will let Marty Mornhinweg help me out on this one: it was a touchdown then, it's a touchdown now, and it's a touchdown 10 years from now.

The 10-second runoff, the batted ball out of the end zone, and now "completing the process." All of these were a farce. If the games were blowouts, with the team far behind, out of playoff contention, etc., then these instances would not be worth mentioning. The blown calls would simply equate to shoveling more dirt on the carcass that is the Lions. Yet, what completely amazes me most about their history is that when they have been jobbed, something of value has most often been at stake, and a complete collapse of their own doing, accorded the rule enforcers to leave them adrift, and rudderless. Seemingly, with not even a life jacket available....

Oh, man... This will not be easy. Many among us will never forget. January 4th, 2015. Detroit at Dallas. NFC wildcard came. The Lions were 11–5 during the regular season. They lost a chance at the division title (and a bye week off) in the regular season finale, to both Green Bay and the Lions' personal tormentor, Aaron Rodgers. The Lions dominated the game throughout the first half. They had a 14–0 lead, with 1:50 left, in the second quarter. Seemingly, even better, was the third down, and the Cowboys were facing 12 yards to go. Showing zero semblance of an offense up until this play, I was hopeful that the Lions could stop Dallas, regain possession, and perhaps get more points themselves before the half ended. Then, it began to happen. WR Terrance Williams caught a short slant pass from Tony Romo, and he went 76 yards for a touchdown without being contacted by as much as a fingernail. While this play is not what the contest is famous for, I will never forget the significance of it.

The course of the game changed from that moment on. That old feeling began to return. Yes, the familiar feeling of watching the same movie, already knowing the ending, yet choosing to sit through it regardless. Matters tightened up, as did the Lions offense. Only two field goals, for six total points, in the second half.

Still, they held on to a 20–17 lead with just over eight minutes remaining, and we were driving when… "it" really happened. Matthew Stafford dropped back and threw a pass to tight end Brandon Pettigrew. An obvious pass interference call, for face guarding and making contact to the receiver before the ball arrived. Yes, a penalty then, now, and 10 years from now.

The flag is thrown. The ball is placed at the spot of the call, and the announcement is made by the official. The drive continues, inside the Dallas 30-yard line. All is good in Lions Land. Then… chaos. Without any explanation, or announcement, an official picks up the ball and returns it to the original line of scrimmage. What was said to then-Lions coach Jim Caldwell, by the referee, as to why the flag was picked up, will remain a mystery.

Stafford, who was mic'd up for the game, had plenty to say to the officials. Just a travesty. However, the piling on, and the disintegration by the Lions themselves, was merely beginning. During the confusion after the play, Cowboys wide receiver Dez Bryant ran onto the field with his helmet off to argue the initial call. THIS action is an automatic, 15-yard, unsportsmanlike penalty. At least, according to the league "coloring book" it is. No flag was thrown on Bryant. I was sickened. If both penalties were enforced, as the football world knows they should have, it would have netted the Lions 30 yards of penalties against Dallas, which would have changed the entire complexion of the game.

Now, with the ball at the original line of scrimmage, it was fourth down, with one yard to go. Caldwell opted to punt. The result of that decision was a shank by the punter, for a grand total of 10 net yards. The piano had been pushed off the roof, and all that remained was the mane of the target below. Given great field position after the punt, Dallas drove for the go-ahead touchdown. On that drive, they converted a fourth down and six, and Detroit committed another defensive penalty, on a third down and seven, allowing the drive to continue. Is that enough consternation for one evening, in such a huge game where the Lions played well enough to win? Not even close. There was an aftermath, as well. President Barack Obama himself spoke out on the reversal of the pass interference call. He publicly questioned why the call was announced, and then reversed, stating that he had not seen that before. I had not either, Mr. President.

And that was because such a mockery of the rules had never occurred in league history. It was the first time an interference call was reversed in NFL playoff history. Only the Lions… Two days after the game, the league admitted that, on the fourth and six play during the Cowboys' winning drive, the stripes missed a "blatant hold" on Dallas, which would have disallowed the play. But, no mention of the reversed call, or of Bryant running onto the field with his helmet off. For this, I say to the league: thank you for your "integrity." Again, is that enough? No, never, not when a citation of the Lions is involved.

After the game, a video surfaced from August of 2014. NFL Vice President of Officiating Dean Blandino was spotted on a "party bus" owned by the Cowboys, with team Vice President Stephen Jones, son of team Owner Jerry Jones. Based on what happened in the game months later, the optics are not good, to say the least. Was there favoritism? Were they close friends? Who can say? A conflict of interest seems plausible. When asked about his party bus appearance and the game, Blandino said that one had nothing to do with the other. What remains certain, is that the entity that Blandino oversees will always be remembered for the controversy that ensued on that January evening of 2015. According to his own words, when talking about the reversed pass interference call, his opinion was that it was a judgement call. I concur. Yes, it WAS a judgement call. Very poor judgement...

It goes without mentioning that the Lions indeed still had the chance to win the game, but they failed on their last drive. I had become accustomed to these failings. It doesn't change that what happened to them that night was just wrong. After the party bus video emerged, it just felt like being Lions fans made us all look like a collective caricature. The piano found its target...

Did the Dallas game have a carry-over effect? Many would argue that the end of one season has no correlation with the beginning of another. I have always disagreed with this belief. The 2014 team was one of the best units Detroit has ever had. With many of the same players returning in 2015, they started the season 0–5...

Chapter 11

Door "Matts"

HOLIDAYS ALWAYS SEEM TO be occasions that the Lions dismantle. Well, often enough! This day, however, brought about the beginning of a franchise being razed to the ground.

It was Christmas Eve, 2000. The 4–11 Chicago Bears sauntered into the Silverdome, their luggage and golf clubs neatly packed, with only warmer destinations in mind. The goal for Detroit? Win the game, make the playoffs. No buildup here. It was "Lionesque" to be certain. Rookie kicker Paul Edinger drilled a 54-yard game-winning field goal, with two seconds left in the game. Yes, the same Mr. Edinger who had made the "take the wind" kick, courtesy of Marty Mornhinweg. Worth mentioning is that Paul Edinger is from Michigan, and he played his college years at Michigan State University. Well, of course he is, and of course he did. There always has to be something noteworthy, aside from the actual result. It's exactly why the Lions fascinate me.

When the kick sailed through the uprights (with plenty to spare), the direction of the franchise took a ghastly turn. It was the longest walk I had EVER taken out of the Silverdome. Not in actual steps paced, but for the trudge, and dejection, that all 80,000 of us felt. The place was a virtual tomb... General Manager Chuck

Schmidt was relieved of his duties, and the Lions hired television and radio broadcaster Matt Millen as president and chief executive officer. No hemming and hawing needed here. His overall record as the GM of Detroit was 31–84. A winning percentage of 27% total. He is widely regarded as one of the worst executives in sports history. He presided over the 0–16 team in 2008. He was fired three games into that season.

When hired by late Owner William Clay Ford, Millen had zero experience working in an NFL front office in any capacity. It was a disaster from the start. The organization fell into ruination. He drafted the previously-mentioned wide receiver, Charles Rogers, with the second overall pick in 2003. One of the worst choices ever, as we know now.

Given a five-year extension in late 2005 by Ford, after four seasons of consistent losing, fan outrage ensued. The "Millen Man March" took place outside of Ford Field. It was a fan protest of the contract extension that was given to Millen by Ford. Losing... had long been the "expectation" in the Motor City. And Millen was far exceeding even that, at a remarkable pace. So, when he was given more time and more money to exact even more destruction, fans reached a fever pitch of frustration.

Millen also had a loathsome encounter with ex-Detroit receiver Johnnie Morton. Released by Millen after the 2001 season, Morton was now a member of the Kansas City Chiefs. In December of 2003, the Lions were blown out by the Chiefs. After the game, Millen was outside the Kansas City locker room. When Morton walked by, the two had an exchange, and Millen called him a "faggot."[24][25] Not a smart move. Why don't you tell us what you really think, Matt?

During the 2010 NFL draft, Millen was on air with Former Eagles QB Ron Jaworski. Somehow, they ended up in a conversation about food items. Millen said, "Ask any Polack from Buffalo how they like them, right, Jaws?"[26] Another display of being unable to read a room. No longer the GM of Detroit, he still managed to make headlines at a draft, by making an absurd choice, albeit not as an executive who was selecting a player. What a dumpster fire… The failures of Millen are well documented. I could fill many pages. Redemption for his historically awful stint in Motown, and his habit of public diarrhea of the mouth? Let us attempt to dredge up something.

When taking the job with Detroit, he admitted to owner William Clay Ford that he had no knowledge or experience on how to build a successful football team,[27] according to a March 3, 2019 article by Don Drysdale for Detroit Sports Nation entitled, "REPORT: Matt Millen says he warned Detroit Lions' owner William Clay Ford." Millen also warned of an uphill struggle, with a steep learning curve ahead.[28]

Years later, long after leaving Detroit, he said during an ESPN interview that he never should have taken the position because of his lack of experience. He mentioned feeling bad for Detroit football fans because he was unable to deliver on what they were hoping for—a winning team.[29]

After returning to the broadcast booth, he actually apologized firsthand to Detroit fans, during a game, on air. His sense of humor came through as well, while speaking about his time with the team. He admitted to making a mistake in having a dream that he could successfully lead a football team.[30] He also apologized to Morton and Jaworski, for his insults towards them.[31] The man admitted his failures publicly, which is admirable. Millen was a great and accomplished player. His 12-year career netted him four Super Bowl rings. He was also, in my opinion, a superb analyst while in the broadcast booth. Which is exactly where all of us Lions fans wish he would have stayed.

I sincerely wish him the best of everything. Health, happiness, and prosperity.

*** Interesting thought… If Edinger had missed the field goal that prompted the hiring of Millen, then Interim Coach Gary Moeller, who replaced Bobby Ross after he quit, would CERTAINLY have been given the head coaching job, with a playoff appearance under his belt. And the front office would have remained intact as well. What would the franchise have looked like for the next eight years in that scenario and beyond? ***

When Matthew Stafford was the first overall choice of the 2009 draft, it was foreshadowed by new Lions Coach Jim Schwartz when he said during a widely reported press conference that the time may have come to replace Bobby Layne.[32] And it was no secret that the team had long been lacking a suitable field general.

I am always going to be a Stafford supporter. He was easily the best QB I have ever seen play for the Lions for an extended period of time. Did he have his share of failures? Did he come up short in big games? Without question, yes, he did. No division titles, and three playoff appearances, all of which were losses. Twice, first in 2014, and then in 2016, Stafford faced Green Bay in the season finale, with the division title on the line, and lost both times to Aaron Rodgers. Rodgers, who dominated the division for many years, broke his clavicle in October of 2017, which caused him to miss the remainder of the season.

Ineptly, and as is customary, Stafford and the Lions could not even sniff at the division title, despite the absence of Rodgers. Many times, in his years in Detroit, Stafford was outplayed by inferior quarterbacks. In totality, he came up short of delivering anything consequential as the on-field leader. And much was hoped for. Does he shoulder the blame for the uninterrupted losing streak of the franchise? Not even close. He never had a running game to support him.

The Lions had exactly one 1,000-yard rusher in his 12 seasons as the Lions QB. That was Reggie Bush, who just barely went over the magical mark, with 1,006 in 2013. He had to endure changing offensive coordinators four times in that 12-year span. Not exactly what I would describe as continuity.

Supporting your franchise QB starts at the top, in the front office, and trickles down to the people constructing the team on the field. And the Lions never put enough overall talent around him on a consistent basis. There were also three different head coaches, one of which fittingly serves as the poster child for the sleight of words to this chapter.

Stafford's career-passing statistical yardage is among the best in league history, largely because of the attempt volume. This was necessitated by the lack of a ground game complementing him, and from being behind in games, playing in catch up mode. The guy is as tough as nails, and he played through many injuries. The one I remember most was in his rookie year. On the final play of regulation, Stafford was struck by Cleveland defensive tackle C.J. Mosely. It remains one of the most vicious hits I have ever witnessed.

Mic'd up for the game on live television, and laying on the ground with his shoulder dangling, he yelled at a teammate who was trying to help him up to get "the eff" off him.[33] The pass was incomplete, but a penalty on the Browns extended the game for one more play. By rule, Stafford had to leave the game for at least one play. But when Cleveland called a time out, that was the respite needed for him to reenter the game and throw the touchdown pass that tied the game. Jason Hanson won the game with the extra point.

During the time out, Stafford lobbied to get back in the game, though obviously in extreme pain, laying on the ground for much of the stoppage. The coaches were yelling "No!" when Stafford asked to return.[34]

His retort? That he could still throw the football if his team needed him to do so.[35]

And that he did. Still very much in pain when the game ended, he had endeared himself to the city, at least for that day. His career record as a Lion was 74-90-1. They would have been drastically worse without him. Traded in the off-season before the 2021 campaign (at his request), he won the Super Bowl in his first season as the Los Angeles Rams signal caller. INSTANT success after ridding himself of the Lions. Just another indictment of the harrowing organization the Lions WERE. Yes, past tense. We are getting there…

When all is said and done, and his playing days are over, Stafford will be a Hall of Famer, and he will rank in the top 10 in many categories. He was always more than serviceable as a leader and as a QB. It merely took a roster of more talented players around him to get him over the top. Not to be underestimated was his character.

There was never an instance where he spoke poorly of a teammate, or coach, when standing in front of a microphone. In private? Nobody knows. That would be their business. I doubt anyone would have blamed him for ripping a game plan by a coach, or a listless performance by a teammate, out of the view of the public eye. He unequivocally took his share of the blame after many losses. His philanthropic contributions have helped change the lives of many families in the city of Detroit. Even after leaving the Lions, he and his wife came back to the city to donate more. And funds were not the only form of support that he gave to Detroit. He gave his time to inner-city youth, interacting with them and helping to uplift the city as a whole.

When he arrived in 2009, Detroit was in very bad shape. The auto industry was having a decided downturn. People were losing their homes, crime was rampant, etc. Just a very bad time here. Stafford embraced Detroit. Made it his home. In times of reflection, while attempting to pinpoint a glimmer of light amidst the darkness, Matthew Stafford provided a break in the clouds, so to speak.

Matt Patricia (2018-2020)

Yes, the coach who was omitted earlier. Time to come off the top turnbuckle. The stench that this guy brought with him, and left behind, throughout the franchise, is unlike any other, even while comparing it to all of the losing that the Lions have done. Hired by Bob Quinn, the two had a long history, while working together for the New England Patriots. It was very predictable as to whom Quinn would hire after firing Caldwell. Patricia was the defensive coordinator of the Patriots. In 2017, before coming to the Lions, the defense that he led was among the worst in the league, averaging a total of 366 yards allowed per game. Only three other teams gave up more, on a game-by-game metric. Even the Lions had a better average.

Patricia's defenses (2012–2017) benefited heavily by playing from ahead, due to the potent offense led by, of course, Tom

Brady. In the 2018 Super Bowl (2017 season), Brady threw for 505 yards, with three touchdowns, and no interceptions. The Patriots added more than 100 rushing yards and another touchdown on the ground. Obviously, plenty of offense to win a football game. Based on those numbers, just another Patriots championship? Yes, but this mountain of offense was barely enough to overcome the "efforts" of one Matt Patricia. I watched in amazement as the Eagles tore through the defense crafted by Patricia. At the very end of the first half, the Eagles scored on a trick play, with QB Nick Foles receiving the touchdown pass from tight end Trey Burton. A great call by Philadelphia Coach Doug Pederson.

I do not recall a defense looking more lost, and unprepared, in my life. At least, not in a singular game. No, not even the Lions. The second half was close throughout, with the Patriots eventually taking the lead in the fourth quarter. Because the game was nip and tuck, the Eagles were able to maintain a great mix of run and pass. Which meant that Patricia had to actually come up with a plan to stop a BALANCED attack. And, true to form, he failed to do so. My initial impression that stuck during and after the game was, "THIS is the guy who the Lions are going to hire?" Right on schedule, and much like a Mike Tyson punch to the jaw, my lifetime-malaise fandom continued, when the very next day after the Super Bowl, Patricia was named head coach of the Detroit Lions. From his initial press conference, I just had a premonition about him.

Before the team ever played a game under his "guidance," a "Lions only" omen came to fruition. After his hiring, it was discovered in May that Patricia had been indicted for rape in 1996.[36]

An August 20, 2018, *Detroit News* article entitled "Lions' Matt Patricia Jailed 20 Hours After 1996 Spring Break Sexual Assault

Arrest" by Francis X. Donnelly reported that Patricia and another person with him were neither tried nor convicted before the accuser ceased cooperation with the prosecutors. The case was dismissed. It's all public record.

The team released a statement saying that Patricia had been the subject of a standard background check, which had not revealed the allegation. Just wonderful. When Patricia himself was quizzed as to why the alleged incident had never surfaced during the interview process, he said during a press conference[37] that the issue had never come up because it had been dismissed. Thanks for that, Matt. Whatever happened, or didn't happen, only three people will ever know. Regarding the indictment, I will always feel that he was not forthright, and conversely, that management dropped the ball by not doing their homework. A true match made in heaven. They deserved one another.

After the reports surfaced, his former Patriots organization also released a statement, claiming that they had also been unaware of the allegations at the time that they had employed Patricia. Not a great start for Mr. Patricia, you may be thinking? Actually, by retaining his job after talking with the team, and speaking hurriedly at a thrown-together press conference, this incident was undoubtably the most success that he experienced as the Lions' head coach. And the only person who benefited from all of it… was him. Quite the blemish.

Returning to the football-related antics, his debut as head coach in 2018 came on Monday Night Football. The Lions lost the game by a score of 48–17. A few exhilarating details are as follows: the Jets rookie starting QB, Sam Darnold, set another record against the Lions. The final margin of 31 points was (and is) the largest ever realized by a rookie QB of his age making his first start. He was the youngest to start a game since the AFL-NFL merger in 1966. The 48 points scored by the Jets were a franchise record for a road game. The 31 third quarter points were a franchise record, and they were scored consecutively and unanswered by Patricia and his new team.

I have not looked to see if since this game, the Jets have surpassed these eye-popping totals in any other contest. However, I would run to a betting window, in support of the New York Jets not having done so. You get the gist of the outcome. The portrait is very vivid. Thank you very much for that historically abysmal evening, Mr. Patricia.

Prior to arriving to the Lions, he largely rode the coattails of Brady, as well as Head Coach Bill Belichick. They were the two main components for the success of the Patriots for many years. On his own with Detroit, he fell on his face. Demanding of his players, Patricia was routinely late for meetings that he himself had scheduled, according to an anonymous ex-Lion. This was reported in an article by Dave Birkett in the *Detroit Free Press* entitled, "Matt Patricia consistently late to team meetings, ex-Detroit Lion says," on December 26, 2018.[38]

The same applied with media sessions, which were very public and required zero anonymity. At one such session, he told a reporter to "sit up," as described in a November 1, 2018, *Detroit Free Press* article by Shawn Windsor entitled, "Matt Patricia's condescending tone would sound better if he was winning."[39] The article goes on to say that Patricia told the reporter to "have a little respect for the process" before being asked a question. Respect for the process? Are you kidding me? This of course, coming from an individual who was late for these same weekly press conferences. I believe there is a word to describe such behavior: pompous. He did have many undistinguished moments to his credit, without a doubt.

I want to be fair, give credit where it is due, and "respect the process." Led by Patricia, the Lions blew no less than 10 fourth-quarter leads, while only coaching in 43 games. Under his brilliance, they also lost nine games while holding a double-digit lead. The 11-game losing streak, at the end of 2019, and continuing into 2020, is the third longest in team history. Only third worst, Matt? Perhaps you could have tried harder to "reach the top!"

When asked by ESPN's Mike Rothstein about his coaching in game situations, Patricia retorted that he was proud of having perhaps one of the biggest fourth-quarter plays in the NFL's history, according to a September 14, 2020, prideofdetroit.com article by Mike Payton entitled, "Matt Patricia's tone-deaf response to Lions' fourth quarter woes is embarrassing" with a sub headline: "Patricia's tone-deaf comment shows how unaware he is of his issues."[40] In this instance, I simply have to grab the low-hanging fruit. The play that Patricia was referring to, was the interception at the goal line, which saved the Super Bowl for New England on February 1st, 2015.

Here are some facts: the Seahawks began their drive at their own 25-yard line, with two minutes and two seconds remaining in the game. Essentially, it was a two-minute drill. Six plays later, the ball rested on the New England one-yard line. So, to be clear, HIS defensive play calling failed the team, to even allow the Seahawks to be in a position to win the game. He was, after all, the defensive coordinator. It was his blueprint.

Then, the Seattle coaching staff made probably the worst play call in the history of this illustrious game. On second down, they decided to throw the ball, instead of handing it to Marshawn Lynch, whose punishing style of running was an issue for New England all evening. Malcom Butler undercut the route and intercepted the ball, ending the game. With 26 seconds remaining, and a time out still in their pocket, it is universally agreed that Seattle should have run the ball with Lynch. Even if the rushing attempt would have failed, they could have used the time out to regroup and have two more plays to win the game.

I was astonished while trying to make sense of this play call. For Malcolm Butler, a career moment. Right place, at the right time. However, the reality is that Patricia was not even the coach who sent Butler into the game. That was Brian Flores, who can be seen in a video yelling to Butler, "Malcolm, go!" on a February 5, 2015 upload on Nick Barajas' YouTube channel entitled, "Brian Flores Patriots coach sends Malcolm in game MALCOLM GO."[41]

And NOT at the direction of one Matt Patricia. So, for him to take any credit whatsoever is presenting himself as delusional. Yes Matt, you drew it up, called the play, and are the one responsible for making it happen. Sign me up to reside on that cloud... Players could not stand the guy. This fact is also well documented. I could give many examples, but I will keep it to a minimum. One such performer was Pro Bowl performer Darius Slay. Unhappy with the defensive scheme implemented by Patricia, the two clashed often.

Slay spoke on multiple media platforms about the rift between the two, as described in a March 19, 2020 *Detroit Free Press* article by Dave Birkett entitled, "Darius Slay: I don't respect Detroit Lions' Matt Patricia because of 2018 incident."[42]

Slay also spoke about how the relationship deteriorated as early as the first training camp under Patricia in 2018. He mentioned how Patricia acted if he were better than everyone. Yes, Darius, even coming from myself, a person who has luckily never had to encounter Patricia, I can certainly see (quite clearly) him giving off that vibe. Amen, brother. Your career took a positive turn when you were rid of him and sent to Philadelphia.

When GM Quinn and Patricia were fired together, two days after the 2020 Thanksgiving Day loss, players from past and present rejoiced. Both were mocked by players in tweets. This reiterated just how disliked both of them were. The two were thick as thieves, and one cannot be mentioned without the other. As a fan, I was overjoyed for the fumigation to begin. For Quinn, 18 of his 31 wins as GM came from the head coach that he inherited, and then fired, who was "not good enough." The other 13 came from his hand-picked disaster.

Patricia? In his first year, he finished last in the division. The second year… last. And when he was shown the door before finishing his third and last season? He was comfortably holding court in the cellar again. He barely had more wins than Rod Marinelli, who had to endure a winless campaign. And at least Marinelli was well-respected for his professionalism and work ethic. In 48 games as head coach, he won just 10 games. Patricia, who came from doing things "the Patriot way" won just 13 games, while coaching in 43 games. Congratulations. By sheer numbers, you are not the "worst" coach that the Lions employed. However, for creating a positive culture and building relationships, there will never be another who failed as miserably as you did. If not for the Malcolm Butler interception, the Patriots would have one less trophy in their case, and your defensive tactics would have been the direct result.

To be succinct—you were bailed out. All of the coaches before Patricia were "Lionized." During your brief and disastrous stint, the organization, and us fans, were all YOUR victims.

Chapter 12

Fame and "Mis"fortunes

IF YOU WERE ASKED to choose between watching paint dry on the wall or having a tooth extracted, which would you choose? Neither are very appealing options. At least the extraction provides some type of sensation. So, I have sacredly kept my weekly appointments, with the Lions wielding the instruments of pain. I have sat (and paced) through some follies, that cannot be understood. One such game took place in December of 2015 at Ford Field.

It was a nationally televised, Thursday night matchup against Green Bay, of course including Aaron Rodgers. On the last play of the game, Rodgers heaved a "Hail Mary" pass into the end zone. The prayer was answered, and Richard Rodgers went up and came down with the ball. Game over. Just another ho-hum Lions low-light? Well yes, of course. Still, this embarrassment in particular was very avoidable. It simply came down to the Lions defensive alignment on the final play.

The team only rushed Rodgers with three players. One of those was their nose tackle, Haloti Ngata. This was a player who is built to work in the trenches, to stop the run, but not to chase down a QB with the mobility that Rodgers possessed. Their best pass rusher, Ziggy Ansah, began the play covering a receiver on the outside, as a defensive back would. Ansah let the outside receiver run free, as did another defender on the opposite side of the field, with both drifting away from the line of scrimmage. They both ended up somewhere near the sprinkler system, between Rodgers and the end zone, rendering them useless. That left six defenders in the end zone.

Meanwhile, with only three players rushing him, Rogers was able to scramble and uncork the pass. Time stood still while it was in the air. The receiver (the other Rodgers) tracked the ball before it reached the goal line, realized that no defender was covering him, drifted into the end zone, jumped with his back to the defense, and caught the ball. Where were the six Lions defenders? Every one of them were BEHIND the receiver, with three of them covering nothing and no one. Yes, by themselves. Jubilation for Green Bay, and shock for our team, and the Lions faithful. Often in these situations, the head coach will insert a taller player, and best leaper, to bat down the ball. For the Lions, this was Calvin Johnson. He was not even on the field. After the game, Caldwell told reporters that he thought the Packers were going to attempt to lateral, which was the reason for the formation that he employed. Again, not the best tactician.

Predictably, the play itself is not the entire story. The Hail Mary was only made possible by the play that preceded it. On that attempt, which would have been the last play of the game, the Packers actually DID lateral the ball, several times, before it ended up back in the hands of QB Rodgers. Eventually, (and finally) he was tackled by Devin Taylor, ending the game. Well, sort of. The official threw a flag for a face mask. Personal foul, 15 yards. One more play. While tackling Rodgers, Taylor grazed the facemask with one of his fingers, but tackled him fully with his hand, on the shoulder pad. Unintentional and incidental contact. He never reached for the face mask, nor did he intend to do so. It was a horrible call. The penalty gave Rodgers the extra yardage needed for his throw to reach the end zone. Caldwell should have known that he had the arm strength to now make that distance and adjust his defense accordingly. The next morning, my (at the time) eight-year-old grandson quickly pointed out this painfully obvious situation to me.

Instead of adjusting his defense, Caldwell set the formation for another lateral attempt. Really? Mind numbing. I highlight this particular game, because it encompasses every aspect of the Lions' historical woes. Bad coaching, horrible calls against them, players failing to make a play, and… unparalleled bad luck.

Renowned for their failings, the Lions have long been fodder for columnists and late-night talk show hosts, both national and local, as well as for play-by-play announcers assigned to their games. Then, the bags over our heads during the wretchedness of the 2008 winless season. Yes, infamous, they are… But I never realized how much so, until I watched a television series named "Ozark." In it, one of the characters is a former UAW negotiator, who is on his death bed. When discussing his impending death with the main character, played by the great Jason Bateman, the fictional ex-Detroiter compares dying to watching the Detroit Lions lose. I watched the exchange, stupefied. A wildly popular Netflix show, with a Detroit Lions infusion and insult, melded into the writing. Once in a fog, my awareness had now reached a new height.

The line was penned by "Ozark" writer Ryan Farley, who grew up in Detroit. Thank you for that, Ryan. Sincerely, with zero sarcasm. I NEED to express my gratitude. Regarding the Lions, long dormant was any thought of them, until 1 p.m. each Sunday. Just weekly resignation, while waiting for the lidocaine to numb me, hoping it would prove effective until 4:00 p.m. Until your line awakened me to just how bad matters were. Genius line…

The Lions won the division title in 1993. The playoff game was played at the Silverdome on January 8th, 1994. The game was blacked out locally, because it was not sold out. A playoff game, not on local television? Yes, apathy. A young Brett Favre rolled out to his left, threw across his body, and hit Sterling Sharpe for the third time that day for a touchdown, this time for the game winner, with 55 seconds remaining. Hold on, everyone. Something just flashed past my window… I am back. No worries, that was Sterling Sharpe, who was still running…

Why mention this specific game at this juncture? Feasibly better chronicled earlier? Perhaps, and perhaps not. Two confirmed people who were in attendance on that day were myself, and a younger Ryan Farley, as told in a May 9, 2020 article by ESPN staff writer Michael Rothstein, entitled, "Inspired by dad: How the Detroit Lions made it into 'Ozark'."[43] Thus, I would assume, an inspiration for the line in "Ozark." Infamy, witnessed by many, and attained as only the Lions can. Both on the field and the big screen, as well.

Chapter 13

Where I Am "Coming From"

DETROIT IS A CITY that works hard and plays harder. It has quite a heartbeat, and a soul. It is a melting pot of many ethnicities. I feel fortunate and blessed to have grown up amidst such diversity. Living here has taught me the difference between race and racism. Obviously, the struggles of the city are well documented. Population decreased by well over 50% beginning in the 1960s, up until 2015, according to Wikipedia.[44] This can largely be attributed to the auto industry slumping in the 70s and 80s, because of jobs leaving the country, due to auto importers when Coleman Young was mayor.

Then Mayor Dennis Archer took office and began tremendous revitalization that included construction of three casinos, Comerica Park for the Tigers, and Ford Field for the Lions, among many other developments.

At the same time, developer Dan Gilbert was purchasing and transforming abandoned buildings into gleaming storefronts, office space, and residential units.

Unfortunately, corruption during former Mayor Kwame Kilpatrick's administration (2002-2008)—which ultimately sent him and several of his colleagues to prison—set Detroit back in a major way. He completely raided the proverbial cookie jar. The guy is not even worth these few keystrokes.

When the Super Bowl came to Detroit in February of 2006, our city was not a destination at all. Large banners were draped over the plethora of abandoned buildings. Metaphorically, we simply threw everything laying around the house into closets and swept up. But Detroit can throw a party like no other, and we did just that. The game was a financial boon for the city. In the years after, downtown Detroit began to transform, steadily, yet surely.

It was during the end of the Kilpatrick disaster. Eyes were now on him, and city dollars began to go towards the betterment of the nerve center. Dave Bing, the former Detroit Pistons player and Hall of Famer, became mayor in 2009, and he did great things for the city, helping to continue the upward trend. Mike Duggan, who ran the Detroit Medical Center, then succeeded Bing as mayor. He has made the city a destination for businesses. Yes, Detroit still ranks amongst the worst in the nation for violent crime. However, it should be mentioned that under Mayor Duggan's leadership, and through the efforts of the police force, those statistics are improving. Blighted structures are regularly demolished. The number of parks, recreation centers, (thank you, Matthew Stafford) and other useable spaces are growing. The city has been on the rebound for several years now, but still needs many improvements. The downtown area is vibrant, as are many neighborhoods throughout the city. Yet crime continues to plague many neighborhoods, while the poverty levels hover around 33%.[45]

This is astronomical. Better times are currently taking place, and the resilience of Detroiters characterizes our entire region.

The NFL draft in April of 2024 was a huge success. More than 700,000 fans[46] crowded Campus Martius to witness football history on a specially built stage. It absolutely warmed my heart, and it made me proud to be a native while in attendance at such a first-class event. The draft in Detroit set an all-time NFL record for attendance and inspired rave reviews by many. The city showcased its preparedness, planning, and infrastructure to manage the huge crowds.

The three-day event fueled our city's momentum towards the ongoing revitalization. Sadly, the iconic symbol of the Detroit skyline, the Renaissance Center, is now the subject of demolition talks. We can send men to the moon, but seem unable to find a viable usage for a set of buildings that are entrenched in the history of the city. Visible from many vantage points when entering downtown, it will be difficult to imagine the skyline without the iconic mirrored towers.

Much like the city itself, our sports scene has suffered a monumental drought, leaving fans thirsting for any drop of success. We have a very rich and proud history in this domain. From 1991 until 2016, the Red Wings made 25 straight playoff appearances, with four Stanley Cup Championships, and six overall trips to the finals. The Red Wings legend Steve Yzerman is now running the organization. Under his guidance, and going into his sixth year, the team has yet to reach the playoffs.

The Detroit Pistons have been a benchmark. Beginning in 1984, and extending until 2009, they made the playoffs 21 times, with three championships, and two other trips to the finals. Their last three trips to the postseason, in 2009, 2016, and 2019, all ended in four-game sweeps. The last time that they won an actual GAME in the playoffs was 2008, let alone a series win. Now, they are the laughingstock of the league. In the 2023–2024 season, they were at the franchise's all-time worst at 14–68. They also set the record for consecutive losses in NBA history, with 28 in a row.

Do we all agree that the Matt Millen regime was an abomination? Look no further than exhibit "B," in the form of former Pistons General Manager Troy Weaver. His three-year record with the team is, and will remain, a shocking 54–192. A winning percentage of just under 21%. He "stepped down" from his position in June of 2024. Very classy of the team to allow that verbiage, before politely closing the door in the face of Mr. Weaver. Without question, his version of burning down a franchise is far worse than that of Millen, albeit for a much more condensed period of time.

But this is about football. Much more hype surrounded the hiring of Millen, and much was hoped for. While I was decidedly underwhelmed, the Lions were almost watchable with Bobby Ross as the head coach. Even with an interim coach (Moeller) after Ross quit midseason, the Lions were on the cusp of being a playoff team. When Millen hired Mornhinweg, the immediate result was a 2–14 season, and the vortex had begun. Weaver took over a team that already had its hole unearthed. The shovels were already left lying around the disturbance in the soil. He merely dug further down in the trenches than any person could have imagined, and he buried himself.

Detroit loves good baseball. Almost as much as football. The last decade, however, has been an atrocity. The overall record from 2015 until 2023? 579–772. In baseball, to be almost 200 games under the break-even mark, in a nine-year span, is simply unspeakable. That includes a record of 47–114 in 2019, as well as the worst team in league history, with a record of 43–119 in 2003.

Please do not tell me about teams that played in the late 1800s, when baseball was a different game. Or the New York Mets of 1962, who, in their very first season, were 40–120. The Tigers were an established franchise when they hit rock bottom. With six games remaining in the 2003 season, they were 38–118. Can you say that again? They were 80 games below 0.500!! They finished "with a flurry," winning five of their last six, to achieve 43 total wins.

Prior to 2015, a four-year run of great success. Four straight division titles consecutively, from 2011 through 2014, and a World Series appearance in 2012. A nice blip on the radar screen. Prior to 2011? We can delve back to 1984. The Tigers won the World Series, with perhaps the greatest team in Motown sports history, led by the legend, Sparky Anderson. They started the season 35–5. Beginning in 1985, through 2005, they made a grand total of one playoff appearance in 1987. After that year, 18 more passed until they remarkably made it to the World Series in 2006. After finishing 71–91 in 2005, first year manager Jim Leyland astonishingly took the Tigers to the grand stage. Although they lost to St. Louis, it was a wonderful season. Leyland was also the manager of the 2012 team that made it to the series, where they lost to San Francisco. He remains one of the most accomplished skippers in MLB history, and certainly one of the best overall, regardless of which sport, in the history of Detroit. He is a Hall of Fame inductee, enshrined in 2024.

Management and ownership of Detroit's franchises? The Red Wings and Tigers are owned by the Ilitch Family, known for the Little Caesars Pizza empire. They purchased the hockey team in 1982, and then the baseball team in 1992. The late owner of both franchises, Mike Ilitch, generously spent his money on these in an effort to field winning teams. From 2012 until 2017, the Tigers payroll ranked in the top five, in each of the seasons in that time frame. In 2011, they maintained the 10th highest payroll, which is still well within the top half of the league. And, as we have established, 2011 through 2014 were the best years that the Tigers have had (consecutively) in the modern age of baseball.

After Mike Illitch passed in early 2017, his son Christopher took over operation of the two franchises. Starting with the 2018 season, the payroll plummeted to the bottom half of the spectrum. It was sort of strange that this reduction directly coincided with the emergence of Christopher Ilitch taking over. From that point on, up until 2024, their payroll remains mired in the 10 lowest, in a league with 30 teams.

Hockey is a different dynamic. Unlike baseball, there is a definite, hard salary cap. Player development, and experienced front office management, are vital. And the Red Wings have had that, with Ken Holland as their lead front office executive. During his tenure in Detroit, the Wings won four Stanley Cups in 1997, 1998, 2002, and 2008. In 1997, Holland's title was assistant general manager. That off-season, he became general manager, and the other three championships soon followed. He left Detroit in the spring of 2019, to make way for the hiring of Yzerman. He then went to Edmonton, where in his five years in the same role, the team made two conference final trips, and a jaunt to the Stanley Cup Finals in June of 2024. And here we are, as Detroit sports fans, waiting six years for Yzerman to deliver the semblance of a winner. Since the passing of Mike Ilitch, and now under the guidance of his son, neither the Tigers nor Red Wings have made a singular postseason appearance.

In September of 2017, Little Caesars arena opened. The new home of the Red Wings. The Pistons joined them as tenants, after the closing of the fabled Palace of Auburn Hills, where the team won championships in 1989, 1990, and 2004. Included in that were six straight trips to the Eastern Conference finals (2003-2008). The cost of construction for Little Caesars was originally estimated at around $450 million.[47] When completed, the final cost was nearly double that of the original plan. Who is bearing the brunt of the staggering increase? The taxpayers, of course.

The Ilitch family assured the public of a grand entertainment district at the site, which would include shopping, eateries, and even a hotel. Nearly seven years later, many of the parcels around the stadium remain untouched.[48] But in 2017, when I attended a Kid Rock concert to open the building, there was no issue with a $75–100 price tag to park my car in the garage, or in dirt lots adjacent to the arena. Which, I would surmise, would have gone straight into the vault of the family. I parked further away and walked, but nowhere near the site, which at the time remained a collection of parking garages and abandoned buildings owned by the family.

They were criticized for misleading us. Plain and simple. But they still asked the public for more taxpayer money in 2019, with no visible sign of progress around the arena. As recently as March of 2024, groundbreaking for development around the arena had not yet begun.[49] Deplorable... I enjoy music in the background, while I am penning. Right on schedule, a song from the 80s new wave band, Naked Eyes, is hauntingly presenting itself about "Promises, Promises."[50] I am unabashed when I say that the Ilitches are no local heroes of mine.

More than any other sport in Detroit, basketball has been an afterthought. The owner of the Pistons is billionaire Tom Gores. In June of 2011, Gores purchased the Pistons, along with the company that he founded, named Platinum Equity.[51] It was a 51/49 percent split, with Gores having the majority. In 2015, he purchased the stake of Platinum, becoming the sole owner of the team. His record as owner since the 2011–2012 season? 370–654 going into the 2024-2025 season. Just a moment, everyone. Those numbers are incorrect. Add eight more losses to the grand total, courtesy of the two playoff sweeps in 2016 and 2019.

I know nothing about Gores, other than what is factual. My perception from afar is that his interactions within the day-to-day operations of his team are minimal. The results for over a decade seem to indicate that. He persistently pursued Monty Williams to coach the team for the 2023–2024 season, giving him a six-year, $78-million-dollar deal,[52] the richest in NBA history at the time. Williams turned down the Pistons initially, but Gores kept coming back to him, sweetening the contract, until it was too much for virtually any person to refuse.

At his introductory press conference, Williams openly admitted that he took the job for the money.[53] Wow! Questions regarding monetary issues have long been sidestepped throughout sports history, by both players and coaches, for obvious reasons. His honesty was commendable. His contribution to the team was much less so. One regrettable season, with a franchise worst record, and an all-time league consecutive game losing streak. Yes, I mentioned the season. And yes, Williams was the coach that the franchise walked the plank with. He left the Pistons, and collected the remaining five years on his deal, at an incredible 65 million dollars. From myself,

Gores gets zero credit for wiping the slate clean, and for paying off Williams. But he assumes 100% of the blame for creating the mess to begin with.

If I could put this into spoken words, it would sound something like this:

"Hey... red light coming!"

"Oh, damn... too late to stop!" Yes, asleep at the wheel sums it up, when depicting this franchise, for many years. In the midst of their record-setting losing streak, during a home game, the fans began to chant, "Sell the team!" I watched it on television.

Mr. Gores stated that aside from winning, the team has done a great deal of good in the community. My jaw dropped. Aside from winning?? While Detroit thanks you for your giving nature, Mr. Gores, we as sports fans would also enjoy the gift of a competitive basketball team, for all of our hard-earned dollars that go into supporting your team. Philanthropy is wonderful, but will always remain a separate domain from success on the court. One franchise with two of the worst baseball seasons in history. Another franchise with two new lows, blended into one basketball season. Both of which, along with many other years of losing, have left a sort of detachment from the fanbase. And a third franchise, which has fallen from the hockey elite, with the loyalists waiting for a return to mediocrity. Is the demise of Detroit's entire sports scene becoming more clear?

That leaves us with the Lions, to whom indifference is never the reaction. Only rage. To portend the reign of ownership that correlates with the Ford family, William Clay Ford, Sr., became the owner, on the very same day that President John F. Kennedy was assassinated: November 22nd, 1963. Eye opening, to be sure. Of course, it is in no way the fault of the family, to have this renowned yet cataclysmic day paired with new ownership assuming a sports team. The two are unrelated, yet are intertwined in history. An inauspicious beginning...

We have reviewed the numbers, results, and the revolting fashion in which they have lost games. And it is truly a phenomenon. I am not privy to the reasons why, or the methodology that the Fords have implemented in their business practices. While wishing I were a fly on the wall, I can only look at the timeless unchanged results, take the information at hand, and identify the common denominator. And this hypothesis points only in one direction. I scoff at those who, when engaging me in conversation about the Lions, spew this tired way of thinking: "The Lions suck because they do not spend any money." Shortsighted, and misleading.

The Lions franchise has reshaped their coaching staff too many times, giving sums of money that were in record numbers at the time the contracts were written. Players? Well, there IS a salary cap, limiting how much you can pay, in an effort to fill out an entire roster. Yes, there are creative ways to circumvent this cap, and move dollars around from year to year. Frontloading and backloading money, etc. There are people smarter than me, who are hired to do this exact task. The reality is, however, that every team will lose star players. Essentially, all teams play with the same deck of cards. Ultimately, it will catch up with every NFL team. So when the Lions have lost players due to contract issues, it is not because they are cheap. Just nonsense... Still, it begs the question: why not ever the Lions? And I can only return to the most logical explanation: ownership.

After Clay Ford, Sr., passed away in 2014, his wife, Martha Firestone Ford, assumed the responsibilities of running the team. Names and faces changed once again, but not the results. She fired Team President Tom Lewand, as well as General Manager Martin Mayhew, both of whom were internal holdovers from the Matt Millen era. Largely, the Lions have always promoted from within, playing musical chairs with executives already in place. Then, Firestone hired Bob Quinn, going outside of the organization, seeking a president/GM for the first time since the Matt Millen experiment. She ran the team for the better part of six years, before yielding to her daughter, Sheila Ford Hamp.

And so, we begin to ease our way into the present. In June of 2020, Hamp replaced her mother as principal owner. Long before the official announcement was made, Hamp had been involved with making decisions, working closely alongside her mother. According to Dave Birkett of *the Detroit Free Press,* Hamp signed off on the decision to retain Bob Quinn and his hand-picked coach, Matt Patricia, despite the unraveling that they brought to the team.[54]

I sort of understood the rationale. If she fired the duo upon taking over the team, it would have been only a month until training camp, and the team would have been searching for a new head coach and front office leader. Not a good situation for the franchise, or the new leaders who would be coming in, with little time to prepare for the fast-approaching season. What Hamp actually thought of Quinn and Patricia became quite evident, when they were both fired after the Thanksgiving Day game. Darrell Bevell finished the 2020 season as interim head coach.

As with Barry Sanders, the team had a ridiculous dispute over signing-bonus money, this time with Calvin Johnson. Once again, the Lions handled it in very poor fashion. Johnson was very vocal, public, and candid about his decisions to leave the game, which were the result of his failing health and the constant team upheaval. As with Sanders, Johnson had to repay a portion of his signing bonus to the team. His disdain for that outcome is well known.[55] He wanted the team to repay the money to him before returning to the fraternity in any capacity.

The counteroffer from the Lions? They "kindly" offered him the chance to "work off" the money by making appearances for the team, signing autographs, and the like.[56] How very shortsighted of them. The amount of revenue that Johnson and Sanders created for the Lions is probably astronomical. Their contributions can never be measured by dollars alone. But that is exactly what the team made it about. With two legends such as themselves, you simply do whatever is needed to make the situation right. No questions asked. Who exactly was the responsible party that offered Johnson work, to recoup the signing bonus money that he requested? I am not qualified to comment.

When Hamp took over in June, the franchise was in flux, training camp was barreling down, and the country was in chaos, with COVID in full effect. The 2020 season came, with empty stadiums, and concluded with the GM and head coach being fired before it ended. Now it was January. In just over six months, that is a lot for any owner to deal with initially, experienced or not. Soon thereafter, Hamp had to interview multiple candidates for the two most important positions regarding the football operations. It was imperative that she made the right hires. And she did exactly that. Fast forward to another draft, off-season, featuring free agency for the incoming regime, which we all can conclude that she was immersed in, and anyone would agree that times were hectic for Mrs. Hamp.

Then, August 2021 arrived. Calvin Johnson was inducted into the Hall of Fame. During his speech, he made no mention of the franchise that he spent his entire career with. And we all knew why. Who was in attendance at this event? Sheila Ford Hamp herself. After the enshrinement, the two appeared cordial as they took pictures together that were published in the media. It was clear (to me) that she was making a real effort, to right a wrong. It's not as if the Lions could take the money he requested back and apply it to their current salary cap. Whatever the conversations entailed, they were obviously to the liking of both parties, and soon thereafter, Johnson was thankfully back in the fold. He received his Hall of Fame ring during a halftime ceremony at Ford Field in September of 2021. A great moment for him, and of course, for us fans. He will be inducted into the Lions Ring of Honor during the 2024 season, in late September. Long overdue…

At the ring ceremony for Johnson, Hamp was drowned out by boos coming from the stands. So much so, that Johnson ended up waving his arms in an effort to get them to stop. The disdain from the Ford Field faithful was twofold: for the way that the Lions treated Johnson, and equally for the continued losing on the field. Yes, they dropped the ball in their dealings with such a great and legendary Lion. However, did anyone mouthing off that day really know if it was Hamp who gave the directive to offer "work" for Johnson, or someone else in the room? Just my two cents, from the far outside, looking in. Anecdotal…

Oh… and that ring ceremony day included another historical football milestone. It just happened to be the game when the aforementioned Justin Tucker nailed his 66-yard record-setting field goal to end the game. Good and bad melded together. Same day… same game… and even in the same (booing) moment, with a Lions legend standing next to Hamp, in a moment that should have been just about him. With the Lions, it seems that the football gods (and Bobby Layne) wish it to be such.

So there, you have my born and bred, east side of Detroit relationships (and some experiences) with all of our sports teams. Not exactly fulfilling. Three have been easier to be "casual" with, and the other unending and always toxic.

Before I forget, to Scott Harris, the president of the Tigers: nobody is expecting you to spend Shohei Otani money to improve the team. (Ohtani signed the biggest contract in the history of professional sports—a 10-year, $700 million contract with the Dodgers after the 2023 season.)[57] How about some real major league hitters, while waiting for your core of young players to develop? And, what if these youngsters do NOT become everyday players? What would your alternative plan be then? Keep us fans waiting longer for a consistent winner?

Your handling of the potential deal for Eduardo Rodriguez, at the 2023 trade deadline, was ridiculous. Fans do not need to know the details of what happened behind closed doors. We know the only important factor: you let a commodity, who was not going to sign a deal in Detroit, walk for nothing. Please do better…

Let's brighten the mood. However, before doing so, just a few more tidbits, if I may.

In the 2019 season, in both games against Green Bay, the Lions never trailed at any point, in either game, until both ended with game-winning field goals by the Packers as time expired.

The Lions have overall winning records against just seven other teams all-time, none of which are in their division. Their combined record against those three teams (Minnesota, Green Bay, and Chicago) is an eye-popping 197 up, and 291 on the negative side, as of the end of the 2023 season. One of the seven that they have been successful against is Tampa Bay, whom we have established as the franchise with the worst losing percentage in league history.

Another notable road losing streak is that the Lions lost 21 consecutive games when visiting the Washington, D.C., area, to play the Redskins. This span of this gap lasted from 1939 until 2013. While not as significant as their all-time road losing streak (26 games), or the 24 consecutive years that they lost at Green Bay, it is yet another example of their feeble history.

When Firestone gave up control of the team to her daughter, it was the first such occurrence of having team ownership pass between two women in NFL history. Yes, it was between two women of the same family, but it's still a pretty cool milestone, and I think it is great. Hamp has done a very commendable job making decisions, and with Calvin Johnson, she has successfully bridged one of the bright spots from the past with the present. She hired competent football people and has separated them from the business side, by stepping aside and letting them do their jobs. If criticism is going to be doled out to the organization for the past, it would be reckless to not give credit where it is due. The lineage of ownership no longer matters. The here and now will remain the focus as the organization thrives.

As if I needed further evidence, Bob Seger is wafting in the background, again reminding me that is now time to "Turn the Page."

Chapter 14

Inception

IN JANUARY OF 2021, the Lions hired Dan Campbell as the new head coach, and Brad Holmes as the general manager. In an interesting twist, the incoming GM did not hire Campbell. Both were hired within days of each other by the Lions brass. Campbell first, and then Holmes. Holmes came across the country from the Los Angeles Rams, where he initially served in numerous roles, until becoming Director of College Scouting in 2013. His scouting efforts were vital in building a competitive roster for the Rams. Without a first-round draft pick since 2016, the Rams had been able to remain competitive, logging four straight winning seasons from 2017 until 2020. In this span, their regular season record was an impressive 43–21. This also included three playoff wins, and a trip to the Super Bowl in the 2018 season. His knack for identifying talent in the middle and lower rounds of drafts played a key role in the success of the team.

His first major move for the Lions was trading Matthew Stafford to his old team. We all know what happened in Stafford's first year with the Rams. Just another indictment of how bad things were... again, I digress. In exchange, the Lions received Jared Goff, the Rams' first-round picks in 2022, and 2023, and a third-round pick in the 2021 draft. As an example of his eye for talent, Holmes used that third-round choice to select Ifeatu Melifonwu, a defensive back. After taking a couple of seasons to learn the professional game, he is now a key member of the Lions defense, and he was brought onto the team without spending a high draft choice.

With their own third-round choice, in the same draft, he selected defensive tackle Alim McNeill, a stalwart in the interior of the line. The gem of that particular draft, however, was fourth-round steal Amon-Ra St. Brown. A wide receiver from Southern California, he has worked tirelessly to become one of the premier pass catchers in the league, and a great blocker as well. Identify, draft, and develop. That is the strength of the Lions general manager. I will refrain from naming every player that he has chosen. His drafts in 2022 and 2023 continued to build what is now one of the youngest and most talented rosters in the league. This, of course, was done in collaboration with his head coach, whose input, I would imagine, is very important in the process. What is evident is that both view the big picture in unison. Holmes has also shown a propensity to make shrewd trades, sometimes moving up to target a specific player, or trading back to acquire more draft picks.

Dan Campbell, at his introductory press conference, mentioned many times that he had learned from Sean Payton, while serving on the Saints' coaching staff as assistant head coach, and as tight ends coach, from 2016 until 2020. After Miami fired their coach early in the 2015 season, Campbell finished the season as interim coach, with a record of 5–7. He played for three teams during his career, including the Lions, where he produced career highs in yardage, touchdowns, and average yards per catch, in 2006. I knew little of him when he was hired by the Lions, except for remembering him as a player for the team. After the press conference, however, there would be no forgetting him. Famous for his "bite off a kneecap" quip,[58] and for apologizing for using profanity, it was very easy to decipher his passion for the game and his genuine nature. Unlike the initial vibe many got from Matt Patricia, this was a breath of fresh air.

However, the beginning of his Lions' coaching tenure was all too familiar. Roster construction (or deconstruction) and player evaluation were the focuses of the 2021 season. The team was 0-10-1 before they won their first game, when Goff hit St. Brown with a pass in the end zone, on the last play of the game versus Minnesota. They finished the season a dismal 3-13-1, but went 3–3 in the last six games. Two of the victories were against playoff teams, Arizona and Green Bay. In the Packer game, although Aaron Rodgers only played one half, the Lions actually looked like a proficient team. In the Cardinals game, they blew out a team that was beginning a collapse.

Going into the 2022 season, there was renewed hope, and valid hope at that. But when the Lions started the season at 1–6, the "oh no" bells began to go off in my head, regarding Campbell. Almost universally, because of his game management style, he began to catch criticism. His overall record was 4-19-1. Tough to ignore that. He never lost the team, however. The effort from the players was there, but not the results. With Green Bay invading Ford Field, a 1–7 record seemed like a distinct possibility. That day, something began to happen. Aaron Rodgers threw four straight incompletions from inside the 20-yard line to end the game. The Lions hung on for a hard-fought, 15–9 win. They intercepted Rodgers three times, including one by Aidan Hutchinson, in the Detroit end zone, preventing Green Bay from scoring a touchdown.

From that day going forward, we began to see the transformation of the team. The Lions rallied to a record of 8–8, going into the regular season finale. While losing for his first season and a half, Campbell stood up, answered all the tough (and sometimes stupid) questions, made zero excuses, and kept working. When the team began winning, his demeanor was unchanged. He remained the exact same person. Never did he become cocky, or portray himself as the "smartest guy in the room." His true character came to the forefront, and I have nothing but respect for how he handled the tough times to reach a better place.

For the Lions to make the playoffs, two scenarios had to play out. They needed the Rams to win against Seattle, and then they needed to beat the Packers again themselves. The first part of the equation did not come to fruition. Although not while standing on the same field together, the officials indirectly took their play-off hopes away. Of course, we know that porous officiating runs rampant throughout the league, and not just in games involving Detroit. This was another prime example, and the reverberations were felt throughout the league, but especially here in Motown. League insider Adam Schefter wrote an article after the game, describing how bad it was, and the contest was the worst officiated game of the year. Wonderful acknowledgement, but only one team lost a playoff chance. Yet again, something of significant value was at stake.

One play, however, deserves mention, which without fail... ties in the past to this day in particular.

After blown calls cost the Rams a victory in regulation, overtime ensued, and the zebras had zero interest in redemption. Rams QB Baker Mayfield, filling in for the injured Matthew Stafford (yes, him), threw an interception. After the play, the Seattle defender who intercepted the ball taunted the Rams' sideline. This should have been an automatic 15-yard penalty, forcing the Seahawks to start their drive inside of their own 20-yard line. Instead, they took the better starting point, given to them by the stripes, and ended up kicking the game-winning field goal.

The player who intercepted Mayfield? That would be one Quandre Diggs, who Matt Patricia and Bob Quinn jettisoned out of Detroit, much like they did with Darious Slay, Jr. Diggs was a great player for the Lions, and he bolstered their secondary. Another pro bowler who could not get along with Patricia. Diggs made him look good, for a fleeting moment in time. We recall his wonderful debut, on Monday night football, yes? On the very first play of the game, Diggs intercepted the very first NFL pass ever thrown by Sam Darnold, and he returned it for a touchdown. For 10 seconds, Ford Field rocked. That, of course, concluded the highlights for the evening.

Even worse, was that Bob Quinn only received a fifth-round pick, in return for trading Diggs. They actually gave Seattle a seventh-round pick, along with Diggs. "Quintricia" is their moniker in Detroit sports history. Wow, did they destroy a franchise... Enough about them.

A month later, NFL Commissioner Roger Goodell spoke to the media during the week of the Super Bowl. And of course, he addressed the officiating. While acknowledging that mistakes are sometimes made, his take on the overall state of how games are called was that it has never been better. His head must be somewhere that is not visible to others. And I am not referring to the clouds. Nobody expects perfection, Roger. Many plays and calls are 50-50 and can go either way. It's a fast game, and it's difficult for officials. All anyone is asking is for you to make certain that the OBVIOUS calls are adjudicated properly, so that your league regains some of the credibility that has certainly been lost.

The Rams-Seattle game was played earlier in the day. The only motivation that remained for the Lions was to knock Green Bay out of the playoffs. While no question disappointed with the events of the day, it would have been understandable for the Lions to be less motivated. In lieu of that mindset, Detroit came out in the frigid temperatures and were the more physical team all evening. They imposed their will on Green Bay. They sacked Rodgers twice, knocked him to the ground multiple other times, and harassed him throughout. It was wonderful to witness. In the blistering cold, the Packers managed to allow their hot heads to get the best of them.

Linebacker Quay Walker was ejected for shoving a Lion. However, it was not a player, but rather a member of the training staff, who was attending to an injured D'Andre Swift. Ridiculous. Hyper aggressive, these guys are. The game carried significance for multiple reasons. The Lions, cheated out of a chance to go to the playoffs, showed their growth, toughness, and eliminated the team that had long tormented them. Their overall record was 9–8. Quite a leap from 1–6. It was also the last time Aaron Rodgers wore a Packers uniform. He was traded to the Jets in the off-season. After four plays in the 2023 season opener, he suffered a season-ending injury. During the 2024 off-season, he missed a mandatory team camp to go to Egypt. A nice way to endear yourself to your coaches and teammates…

The last pass he threw at Lambeau Field was an interception by Kirby Joseph, who also picked him off twice in the game at Detroit. In his last three seasons as the field general, Green Bay lost their season finale at home, twice in playoff games, and then to the

Lions. He produced very little offense in any of these games. After his 2021 MVP season, he began to decline. His statistics, and the eye test, told Packers management that it was time. Rodgers and the team "mutually" parted ways,[59] but I imagine they grew weary of his ongoing drama, along with a withering performance.

This is merely my "armchair assessment." He was always quick to blame anyone, or any circumstance, for his failures, but seemingly unable to ever call himself out; I would imagine he became a drain on the organization. When Adam Schefter contacted Rodgers in the off-season regarding his possible trade, Rodgers told him to lose his phone number.[60] And of course, he went on television to proclaim that he had done so. No drama there, whatsoever. Nothing but class. What a guy! It was time to leave behind his version of the "Days of Our Lives" soap opera, take the capital gained from unloading him, and hand the reins to Jordan Love, the QB in waiting. Good riddance.

The loss to the Lions was the proverbial nail in the coffin. It will always remain as one of my favorite games to watch. It was as satisfying as a playoff win, which should tell you all you need to know about being a Lions fan. Detroit had now emerged as the favorite to win the division in 2023. And they slayed a dragon in doing so. I was watching the ongoing construction of an actual football team.

Chapter 15

"The More Things Change"

THE LIONS BEGAN THE 2023 season in the same fashion as they ended 2022. By winning eight of 10 games. Yes, momentum is a very real force, and every effort to maintain it should be emphasized. In the off-season, within the season, and yes, within the confines of a single game. If lost by fate, we can live with and accept that. But by decision making? That is much more difficult to come to terms with. How fleeting it can be; that's the enduring lesson of a truly remarkable campaign.

As Lions nation is well-aware, they clinched the division title on Christmas Eve. Yes, an actual HAPPY holiday, courtesy of the Lions. When it was announced that the Rams would be the playoff matchup, I truly felt a lifetime of football-watching come full circle. Surreal is the only word I can use to describe watching Matthew Stafford come into Ford Field as an opponent. I soaked everything in. All anyone could talk about was his return to Detroit.

However, there was another storyline that I found much more compelling. When Jared Goff was traded to Detroit for Stafford, it had to be tough to swallow. Adjusting to a new city, in which a then-horrible franchise resided. Thrown under the bus[61] by his former coach, Sean McVay, and just two years removed from playing in the Super Bowl. Then, watching Stafford and McVay come together, and win the Super Bowl instantly? Yes, the playoff game was vindication for him. Since his arrival in Detroit, Goff has been a centerpiece in the revival of the franchise. Just a true professional, and a leader.

The game itself lived up to the hype. The Lions won by a single point, on the strength of their usually subpar defense. They held a very good Rams offense, to just six points in the second half. Conversely, the Lions offense, one of the best units in the league, started fast in the first half, as they usually did, but then struggled in the latter stages, which yes... they also did at times during the season. They scored a meager three points in the second half. That lone field goal became a center of controversy as the playoffs continued. Stay tuned...

The entire day of January 14th, 2024, will always be remembered. Along with it being the coldest day that I have ever felt, I was blessed and fortunate to spend it with three people who are most special to me. Need more drama, or higher stakes? Even before the ball was kicked, another potential gift under the tree awaited Detroit fans. With Green Bay upsetting Dallas earlier in the day, it meant that the Lions would play a second home game, if they were to prevail. The aftermath was insane. Strangers hugging, chants of "Let's go, Lions!" reverberating throughout the throng.

With Dallas doing what they always do (choking), it was time to get ready for Tampa. Hilarious sidenote: in a press conference during the week before the game, Buccaneers Head Coach Todd Bowles was asked by a "reporter" if the frigid temperatures in Detroit would affect the performance of his team. Do I really need to deliver a punchline, or a sneering explanation? Just another prime example of why you do not place a microphone, or a camera, into the hands of a person not qualified.

The playoff game against Tampa was another close one. Detroit scored two consecutive touchdowns in the fourth quarter to break a 17–17 tie. When Derrick Barnes intercepted Baker Mayfield, now the QB for the Bucs, to close out the 31–23 win, two events materialized simultaneously. It was Barnes' first career interception, and the first time in franchise history that Detroit had won two HOME playoff games, in the same postseason. Sheer jubilation.

Onward to the NFC Championship game. One win away from… say it with me… the Super Bowl. If any person claims to have envisioned the Lions dominating San Francisco, in the manner in which they did in the first half, I would dismiss that claim quickly. But dominate they did, and not by any accident. A stunning 24–7 lead at halftime. I "told" Campbell from my couch to use the clock, and the solid Detroit running game, to your advantage. Mix run and pass, but do not be overly conservative. Play clean football, do not turn the ball over, and most importantly, take zero unnecessary risks.

Metaphorically, the California ocean view was breathtaking. The winding coastal road was about to take us suffering fans to a destination once thought of as galactical. Unfortunately, the Pacific Coast Highway… has many cliffs. Taking your eyes off the road to enjoy the beauty can and will result into an immediate descent. And at the bottom of one such ravine, is precisely where the Detroit Lions bandwagon ended up that Sunday evening. On the first drive of the second half, Detroit forced the 49ers to kick a field goal. Within the battles of the game, this was a win for the Lions defense.

I was elated. It would also prove to be a very wise and patient move by Kyle Shanahan, the 49ers head coach. 24–10...

After the 49ers' field goal, the Lions drove to the San Francisco 28-yard line, facing a fourth and two. And so, we begin the "second guessing" portion of the show. I must preface before continuing. Dan Campbell is the person most responsible for the transformation of the Lions, in my estimation. He is a master motivator. He will forget more football than I will ever gain knowledge of. I hope he remains the sideline leader for many years to come. I love him as the coach of the Detroit Lions. However, everyone has foibles. Unlike some fans, I will not drink bathwater.

With that in mind, permit me to back up to the late regular season game versus Dallas. This will serve as one last tie-in, to remind everyone that along with any good Lions vibes, trials and tribulations must coincide. The game was massive in its importance, with the winner taking control of the number two seed in the conference, with only one game remaining in the regular season. Down seven, with a minute and 41 seconds remaining in the game, and no time outs, the Lions drove the length of the field and scored the touchdown to cut the lead to one. Only 23 seconds remained.

Immediately, Campbell chose to pass by the tying extra point and go for two to take the lead. I thought this was brilliant even before the result of the play. Detroit had just hit Dallas with a punch to the jaw, with their touchdown drive. Time to deliver the knockout blow. Yes... momentum. As a blocker, and typically never a pass catcher, offensive lineman Taylor Decker reported as an eligible receiver, as required by rule. And he did exactly that. It was now incumbent on the officials to alert the Cowboys defense that Decker was a legal receiver on the play. And they did the exact opposite. Decker caught the pass in the back of the end zone, and the city of Detroit erupted… for about five seconds.

Before my own personal celebration began, I once again scoured the field for the inevitable piece of yellow laundry. It is what I have been conditioned to do. And, lo and behold, there it was. Claiming that Decker never reported as an eligible receiver, the Lions were flagged for illegal touching. So, no celebration of any kind for me. Not even of the premature nature.

Up until this point in our journey, I have yet to mention the role of the officials, in being complicit with the failures of the Lions… I wish I could have watched your reaction to reading that line! With the penalty assessed to Detroit, any two-point conversion would now occur from the seven-yard line, instead of the two. While still shaking my head in disgust, I resigned myself to Detroit kicking the extra point, and taking the game into probable overtime. Too much to ask for? You bet it was. It was then that Campbell made the worst decision that I have seen him make… up until then. He actually sent out his offense for another two-point attempt, from the same seven-yard line. This was hardly the time to go purblind.

The sports-watching nation saw what happened. But now, the football universe was clearly sending another message to you, Mr. Campbell. The chances of being successful again, now from a further distance, and with Dallas now prepared and not teetering, were nanoscopic. Just kick the extra point and prepare to play more football. Dallas still gave him a chance to reign himself in, by committing a pre-snap penalty, moving the ball to the three-and-a-half-yard line. A moment to think about it, perhaps? Yes, a better chance than from the seven-yard line, but simply not the same groove as the first attempt, which caught Dallas off guard. They ran the play, which was an incomplete pass that did not even reach the end zone. Low and off-target, the receiver never had a chance to catch the ball, and then run with it. Just a bad play, and an even worse way to end the game. And this is the enigma that is Dan Campbell. Sharp minded and focused almost always, yet unfettered when there is no need to be. Might this mishap serve as a lesson learned? Let's return to the scene of the crime...

Fourth and two, from the 49ers' 28-yard line. A 24–10 Lions lead. Past the midway point of the third quarter. Campbell passed up the chance for points, to go for it on fourth down. I did not agree with it then, nor will I ever think it was wise. Usually sure-handed receiver Josh Reynolds dropped the pass from Goff. Here is exactly what three points would have accomplished at this critical juncture in the game... going into the NFC Championship, the decided weak link of the Lions was their defense. With two-and-a-half quarters expired, they had relinquished a mere 10 points, against one of the best offensive units in the league. This was an unexpected benefit. A field goal would have restored the 17-point lead that they enjoyed at halftime. What better way to help out a suspect defense than to provide them with more points?

With now only less than a quarter and a half to play, you would have condensed the clock and tightened the noose around the neck of your opposition. San Francisco was beginning to run out of possessions. And with the knowledge that the Lions offense was capable of scoring quickly, and at any time, it is reasonable to assume that they would have begun to drift away from the run game, and become less balanced, thus playing into the hands of the Detroit defense.

Immediately after the Reynolds drop, the demons from the past returned for their haunting. On the second play of the 49ers' ensuing drive, QB Brock Purdy dropped back and uncorked a deep pass. And why not? Their field position was now better than it would have been, with a probable touchback that would have occurred after a field goal by Detroit. Yes, all small details that should be thought out, before the train car begins to disengage from the track. The pass from Purdy hit Lions defender Kindle Vildor squarely in the face mask, as he tumbled to the ground. The ball fluttered in the air, with a multitude of available destinations. The ground would have been the most preferable. Of course, it landed in the hands of wide receiver Brandon Aiyuk, who dove forward and collected it before it hit the ground, inside the five-yard line. Only the Lions...

Three plays later, San Francisco scored again. 24–17. On the first play after the kickoff, sensational rookie Jahmyr Gibbs fumbled the football. I felt terrible for him. He is an electrifying player. On second down, Purdy scrambled 21 yards to inside the Lions' five. It was one of three scrambles by him, that were particularly backbreaking in the second half. Two plays later, they scored. 24–24. Each time that I closed my eyes in pain, the lifetime of flashbacks reappeared.

On the next Lions drive, Reynolds dropped another critical pass, this one on third down, which would have gone for more yardage. San Francisco took the ball, and drove for a field goal that gave them their first lead of the night, with just under 10 minutes remaining in the game. Why every detail? I can explain, or perhaps you have already noticed. Since the decision by Campbell to eschew the field goal, all of these happenings occurred in rapid fire, one drive after the other, with zero break in the petrifying trend. Simply a chain link, with razor wire that connected all of it. Was everything that happened his fault? Of course not. No person could foresee a collapse of such proportions. However, his decision left the door cracked just enough for San Francisco to slip their foot in, and probably prevented it from being closed completely. He allowed momentum to slip away. Still, they had a great chance to stem the tide, get off the deck, and regain their composure. But… why break status quo? Am I paranoid, you may wonder? No, I am not. It is not paranoia when the outcome is always the same.…

The Lions took the ball and drove to the San Francisco 30-yard line. Another fourth down, and two yards to go. Time to stop the bleeding and put the points on the board. Certainly, without any question, the only logical choice was to attempt the field goal and tie the game, agreed? Not in the estimation of the Lions' head coach. Again, they went for the first down. The play was discombobulated as soon as the ball was snapped. Goff rolled out to the right, which is not his forte. He underthrew a sliding St. Brown. One of the worst decisions I have ever seen any coach make, considering the circumstances.

The 49ers took the ball and drove for another long touchdown, featuring one of Purdy's elusive scrambles. 34–24. No break in the chain link. Three minutes remained. A bleak outlook. But Campbell was not finished diminishing the miniscule chance that remained for the Lions. Actually, I am mistaken. He did NOT diminish the small hope that remained. He took it away completely. Or, offensive coordinator Ben Johnson did. Important to be fair. It was one or the other. With a minute and 17 seconds remaining, the Lions had a first down just inside the San Francisco 10-yard line. What was more momentous, were the three time-outs that Detroit had in their pocket. In this situation, the ball most preferably should be thrown into the end zone, once… twice… and if necessary, three consecutive times.

If throwing into the boundaries, the pass catcher getting tackled inbounds was not an option. That would force the Lions to use one of their three golden tickets (time outs) and effectively throw away a precious 40 seconds. They would now only have the ability to stop the clock two more times, after kicking off. On first down, they managed to escape this, by getting out of bounds to stop the clock. The ball now sat at the one-yard line. Incomplete pass on second down. I didn't need to re-research any play in this sequence. Every detail will remain emblazoned in my worst memories.

Third down… Clearly, the one plan that was completely out of the question, on ANY of these three critical plays, was to try and run the football. If unsuccessful, this would also force Detroit into using one of their time-outs.

I did not imagine a scenario in which the Lions' coaching staff would devalue the declining seconds that were available. Each of them should have been treated exactly for their representation, which equated to oxygen. I was hopeful that they would stick to the only remaining blueprint to victory. Lions' life lessons should have told me another story. One third and one, they ran the football. What on earth were the Lions thinking? That they were going to "outsmart" the 49ers? NOT the time to be cute or tricky. San Francisco swallowed it up for a two-yard loss. They were waiting for it. Now, using the first timeout was a foregone conclusion. When play resumed, the Lions scored on fourth down. Just wonderful. Congratulations.

Fifty-six seconds remained. With three timeouts at your disposal, that is an eternity of time in a football game. Especially only trailing by a field goal. With only two stoppages, it equals just 16 seconds, if by some miracle you are able to recover the onside kick. The decision to run on third down was not only wrong, but truly reckless.

There was another critical element that was missed by Campbell. After scoring and keeping the timeouts secured, there would be no need to attempt a desperate onside kick. Detroit could have kicked off deep, with the probable result ending in a touchback. That would mean, no time elapsed from the clock. Squeeze every drop, remember? Then, you begin to use your timeouts, stopping the clock three times, and getting the ball back with 35–40 seconds remaining, after receiving the punt. If the opponent gets a first down to end matters, then so be it. You have to use the time outs at that juncture, regardless. With an offense as capable as the Lions have, that would have been plenty of time to reach field goal range. This is not any type of make-believe screenplay, or figment of my imagination. In 40 years, I have witnessed this exact storyline materialize more times than I have knocked over pins in a bowling game. The miscues by the Lions were not the fault of Campbell in the NFC Championship. But to say that his game management was poor would be an understatement. No officials to blame on this disconsolate evening...

His decisions in past games were major factors, as to why the Lions were winners. There is no questioning that. He has a very keen football acumen. But at times, and in specific situations, being conventional is the prudent thing to do. Simply looking at the advantageous situation that you found yourself in, how the field goals would have benefited the team, and most of all… what was at stake. This was not a regular season game. Analytics? Probabilities? Many say that these are what drive coaching decisions in the NFL of today. These metrics should be considered a manual, or guide, for what to do in CERTAIN situations. But never should they serve as the final answer.

The field goal kicker that Campbell chose NOT to trot out for the potential critical points-twice? That would be Michael Badgley, who just two weeks earlier, had provided the Lions their only points in the second half against the Rams. That effort was a 54-yard field goal. He saved their season. Yes, it was indoors. I get that. However, if a kicker cannot make field goals from 45 and 48 yards, on a 65-degree night, with zero wind or rain, then said kicker should not stand on the sidelines, wearing a uniform. Not compelling enough? In two seasons with Detroit, he made 24 out of 28 attempts in the regular season. In addition, all three of his post-season tries were true. I have never been mistaken for a mathematician, but I believe that equates to a success rate of 27 out of 31 field goals made, for a percentage of just over 87%. To those who believe that Campbell can do no wrong, there is a "probability" for your ass. Would you like icing on your cake?

Going into the game, 49ers Coach Kyle Shanahan's career record when trailing by 17 points in the second half was 0–19. I ask of you to do some math sleuthing of your own and try to deduce what his dossier stands at now, in such situations. Literally only the Lions. Unlike the other three major sports, where baskets, runs, and goals happen as they happen, football is not about choosing to subtract viable points in the most important moments. We all hoped that Campbell learned a lesson from trying for multiple two-point conversions against Dallas. Again, the first attempt was the right call, at the right time, and the best example of why we love him. But lining up to go for it from the seven-yard line, after the Lions were robbed? Just… no.

On the last play of the first half against San Francisco, Campbell chose to kick a short field goal, instead of trying to score a touchdown from the three-yard line. This decision gave the Lions their 17-point lead. Strangely conservative for him. In my mind, however, it was the right move to make. Quite the chasm between that choice, and what he did in the second half. Shanahan, as we remember, took three points at the onset of the second half. Again, this conclusion on his part was the difference in the outcome.

A question for my fellow Lions fans: what was your favorite development of the Lions' off-season, heading into the 2024 season? A player who was drafted, or signed in free agency? The continuity maintained, by both the offensive and defensive coordinators returning? How about resigning their key players to long-term extensions?

Mine does not include any of the aforementioned. Drum roll, please. When Campbell told a radio station[62] that he was willing to dial back on his aggressive game management style, that to me was the most significant happening of the summer (football related, of course). When he took over in 2021, the Lions had one of the worst teams in the league. Taking radical chances throughout games was really the only way that they would have a chance to win. With the metamorphosis of the roster, this type of risk taking is no longer needed. He can now have more trust in the players, but still not lose his propensity to catch teams off guard, when the situation and the feel of the game dictate that. In no way do any of us want him to change his basic approach. Just to be more situationally aware, and to not let emotions guide his choices.

Of course, the needless onside kick failed. Game over, Super Bowl vaporized. Initially, I was in a nebulous state. A sleepless night. As daybreak arrived, indignance took over. And eventually, I became coherent. A long-awaited magical season. Division champions. Defeating Matthew Stafford in the playoffs. A historical second home playoff victory. A ride that none of us wanted to end. It was enchantment. Then, whisked away like pixie dust. Stealing my brother's car when I was 17, and taking it for a drive, was the only event that was comparable, in terms of exultation. Yes, everything changed in 2023. However, rock legends Led Zeppelin continue to hauntingly remind us that "The Song Remains the Same." [63]

Chapter 16

That Time of the Year

FOOTBALL IS A WONDERFUL, tactical sport. The strategies involved intrigue me. A week of game planning to exploit the weaknesses of your opponent. Disguising your scheme and showing a different look to hide your true intent, are reasons why it is such a chess match. It is the part of the game that I most enjoy.

It is unquestionably the most popular of the four major sports, by a wide margin. I have only ever been interested in what happens between the lines each Sunday. Other than the stars whose images are plastered on billboards, or who are frequently interviewed on television, I honestly would not know what these guys look like with their helmets off. And I would take a gander that the players would prefer it that way, at least on occasion. When people fawn over the players by approaching them in public while they are simply trying to enjoy a meal with family or friends, it must be annoying.

I love the game for what it is. There is zero "bromance" from myself towards the players. They entertain me with their immense talent, and that is all that I expect from them. They do not need to feel obligated to sign a napkin from my table in a restaurant. I do not wear jerseys with the name of a player on it. And here is a perfect example of why…

A guy called in to a local radio station. Yes, I was listening. He was having a beer downtown, after a Red Wings game, in the heyday of the team's success. And who walks into the bar? The player whose jersey he was wearing. The guy said that in the moment, he wanted to crawl into a hole. And I would have felt the same way. I give him credit for being so forthcoming.

Adoration should be left for kids, or perhaps women who have a crush on a player. But that is just how I roll personally. To each their own. I fully realize that I am in the vast minority. The bulk of my Lions gear represents the old "dot" logo from years past. I simply love tradition. And perhaps the team has now begun to implement a new custom, which is called winning.

The Lions are now not only a local hit, but a sort of national frenzy has developed as well. Or, as the great classic rock band INXS so aptly described it, a "New Sensation."

I have traveled to 13 different cities to watch the Lions play road games. Until 2023, when I went to Tampa, they won exactly once. That victory was on September 12th, 2004, in Chicago. I mentioned the Lions' record 26 road game losing streak from 2007 until 2010. Going into the game in Chicago, the Lions were working on another streak. They had lost 24 consecutive road games, going winless away from home for three straight seasons, from 2001 through 2003. This streak ranks as the third worst in league history, behind their own record of 26, and just slightly better than the Cleveland Browns, who dropped 25 straight road tilts from 2015-2018. Again, pardon me for drifting. But yes, our Lions have spent many seasons playing in a "league of their own!!"

Back to the 2004 contest. On that day, the Lions broke the 24-game losing streak for road games, on the strength of a blocked field goal, which was returned for a touchdown in the third quarter. Sad to admit that this was one of my greatest triumphs as a fan of the team. There may have been perhaps 100 fans there, representing the Lions. In Tampa in 2023, a Lions throng took over the stadium. I simply ask, *Where were all of you "fans" for the baker's dozen of games that were truly embarrassing to attend?*

Anyone and everyone is a Lions fan these days. They are the new hip and cool item in the league.

I worked with a guy for more than a decade, who bashed me daily for being a supporter of the team.

And NOT in a joking nature. He hated their existence, and called me a variety of names for watching and attending games. He stated that he would NEVER waste a moment of his life on the Lions, regardless of whether they were good or not. According to him, he would not go to a game, even if he were given tickets. His reasoning was solely the management of the team.

Then, big surprise. At halftime of a game in 2023, I went to the concession stand for a beverage. And can you guess who was standing in line? Yes, he and his wife and child, decked out in Lions garb, head to toe. And, to make matters worse from my old school perspective, he was proudly wearing a jersey with the name of a current Lions star on his torso. We locked eyes, and he quickly and knowingly looked away. I just shook my head and grinned. What a very small world, and what a very disingenuous person.

There are many "fans" like him in Metro Detroit. They now call in to local radio stations, giving their "resumes" to prove they are a Lions fan, including: length of time they have watched, games they went to, how much they suffered, etc. And being a long-time listener of said radio stations, I unequivocally recognize them as the same people, who had once called in to state what fools those of us were, for continuing to watch, or attend games. You cannot stop people from jumping on the bandwagon.

But to those who are merely frontrunners—look in the mirror and know who you are. I am NOT portraying myself as the "driver" of the Lions bus/bandwagon, making the decision of who is (and not) allowed to climb aboard. My ego has never been that large. I have unhappily worn the dunce cap for more than four decades, waiting for ownership of the "vehicle" to get it running at optimal level. Now that it is humming along nicely, standing room is not even available. I am happy to merely enjoy the ride, knowing that I have paid my "fare" in full, both figuratively and literally.

Myself? I have routinely gone into stupors from the Sunday night after a game, until the next exercise in futility seven days later. I lick my wounds, and come back for another pounding, just looking for a glimmer of hope that may lead to something tangible. This is why the current success of the team is so personally satisfying to me, and to the millions of other true fans who have languished.

I was lucky enough to be invited to a suite for a few games in 2023. There, I met a very nice (and drunk) guy, who was even luckier, because he got to accompany the team on a trip to a road game. While there, he told me of an encounter he had. He went into the bathroom to take care of business, and standing in the urinal next to him was one of the star Lions players. He was very descriptive, and evidently very fulfilled from having stumbled into this "meeting."

So much so, that he proceeded to tell me the story TWICE during the game. My two takeaways from the tale? I hope that he had looked straight ahead for the duration, and not sideways, over the partition. And that he did so without starting a conversation. Uncomfortable! And finally, did this experience provide some type of "enhancement" in his life? Wow. Have another drink, dude.

The appeal of the NFL is not just within the borders of our country. The game has been an international success as well. The league has routinely played regular season games overseas since 2007. Some of the destinations have been England, Canada, Mexico, Germany, and in 2024, Brazil. Having a football franchise in your city is very beneficial in many ways. The charitable work and donations that teams provide, can simply change lives. For as long as I can remember, the Lions do great and inspiring things in Metro Detroit.

Speaking of international borders, I need to mention my lone sports hero. His name was Pat Tillman. He played for the Arizona Cardinals. He gave up riches and fame to join the U.S. Army Rangers and defend our country while in the prime of his NFL career. Would I have done this? No, never. He was more of a man than most who have walked the earth. While in Afghanistan, he was killed by—of all things—friendly fire. Tragic and sad.

And what thank you did he, his family, and the soldiers who fought alongside him receive? The Army lied to his family about how he died, claiming that the enemy had shot him, to protect their image.[64] There is also a documentary with interviews of other men who fought alongside Tillman. They claim that they were discouraged from telling the truth and asked to participate in a massive cover up. Do I believe them? Damn right, I do. The entire truth eventually came out. Despicable.

The presidential administration at the time was complicit in the scandal, as well. Oh… I have to add that they were ALLEGEDLY involved. Yeh, okay. Sadly, that is the truth about the leaders of our country, then and now. Republican or Democrat, it has no bearing. For myself, too many are self-serving, and only loyal to the few in their inner circles or cliques. They threw a hero who sacrificed EVERYTHING under the bus and caused his family and fellow soldiers to have long-lasting mental anguish. That was cowardly and typical.

For as entertaining as NFL games can be, enough can be enough.

The league plays on Sundays, Monday nights, Thursday nights, and near the end of the season, Saturdays. In 2024, the Packers and the Eagles will open their season on a Friday night. Is a Wednesday night tilt in our near future? Well, as it turns out… yes. Kansas City, Houston, Baltimore, and Pittsburgh will play games on Saturday, December 21st. And all four teams will turn around and play only FOUR days later, on Christmas day. "Player safety," you say, Mr. Goodell? Fraudulent…

In the off season, draft rumors begin immediately after the Super Bowl. Then comes the draft itself, and grading the drafts of each team ensues. Which is another ludicrous exercise, when no one knows what the career paths of these players will be for years.

Then comes off season mini camps, mandatory camps, and eventually, training camps in late July.

It is true saturation. It comes at us 365 days a year. And the league knows they have you hooked. Why not just drop a blimp over my home, with advertisements silhouetted and rotated, much like the Sphere in Las Vegas? The league can certainly afford it. But yes, I do mark the first game of each season on my calendar, to witness which creation of the Lions presents itself.

I often daydream about what the city would become if the team actually made it to the big game. I harken back to the championship parades and the celebrations that the other teams provided for us, long ago. The parades took place on Woodward Avenue, the main drag through Downtown Detroit. If the Lions participated in the Super Bowl, a large thoroughfare would fall far short of accommodating the overflow. The freeway system would need to be cleared. A day off (or two) for a local holiday? No, sir and ma'am. More appropriate would be a full seven days.

Simply put, the Detroit Lions winning the Super Bowl would truly be a once in a lifetime thrill. Will it happen? Let's delve into that possibility. As we know, the Lions made it to the NFC Championship game in 2023 and lost. The last team to reach that point, lose in that round, and make the Super Bowl the next season, were the Packers in 1996. Going into the 2024 season, and for THIRTY-FOUR years consecutively prior to 2024, at least four teams that had made the playoffs the previous season, failed to qualify the following year. These are strong trends.

However, the Lions, under Brad Holmes and Dan Campbell, have been reversing the trends that have imposed their will on the franchise. I am just thankful that I have a reason to watch every week. My quest for football validation is not very far reaching. Just give me a competitive, competent team to watch every week.

One bad bounce of the ball, an untimely injury to a key player, or more likely, a horrible call by an official, are all circumstances that can derail a promising season, while batting an eyelash. The league is very competitive, and any team can beat you on any Sunday. My watching history has told me that WHEN you play a certain team, is more telling than WHO you are playing. You can reach the top of the mountain quickly, and take a tumble down just as rapidly.

A popular acronym for the NFL is "Not For Long." Case in point: In 2022, the Philadelphia Eagles made a trip to the Super Bowl. In 2023, they started the season with a record of 10-1. They then proceeded to lose six of their last seven games, finishing with a blowout loss to Tampa Bay in the playoffs. I can only imagine how mortified Darious Slay was, when of all people, Matt Patricia was given the autonomy to take over the defensive play calling late in the season, in a futile effort to plug holes into a sinking ship. To the Eagles' head coach, Nick Sirianni—*what were you thinking?*

I miss Stuart Scott of ESPN for his genuine nature and hilarious commentary. Too many after him attempt to be funny, but simply are not. Annoying is a more accurate description. Thank goodness for some of the remaining holdovers, who are talented and informative. Those include Hannah Storm, Stan Verrett, and Linda Cohn, to name a few.

Speaking of annoyance, why is it that when I attend a concert, someone feels the need to blare the music of the artist that will be performing, in the parking lot while tailgating? I am well aware of what my ears will be taking in for two hours that evening. Can we allow the pot to simmer, and ease into it? Just had to mention that. I also have to reiterate my strong dislike for what the "college" football game has become. Players no longer go to schools because it was their childhood dream. They have zero affiliation with (or adoration for) the institution. It is strictly for the money. It is a train that is quickly coming off the tracks. I will not be in its path. I have stepped away completely.

Soon, high school players will be offered more money to play at a school, than an NFL player who has played out his first professional contract. Traditions and rivalries have gone by the wayside. No thank you.

Well, it is late August. The calendar is about to shift into fall. Time to hunker down and soak in my own version of a daytime soap opera—the 2024 NFL season. While I have to endure the weekly hype train of cameramen following a player to and from his hotel, getting off the team bus, and creating a blog about what attire they are wearing, I will fervently be watching our team, to see if they can recreate the magic of 2023.

As for the 2024 season, I will not chronicle a single play. It will remain a blank canvas, leaving the Lions to write and illustrate their own story upon it. Because of my hunch that it may be a special campaign, it would only be fitting that the players and coaches tell the story with their performance on the field. Let us reconvene during the playoffs in January, for which I will make my lone prediction for the 2024 season, and feel assured in saying that the Lions will be participants.

Before I appeal to the gatekeeper of the "curse," may I offer you some GOOD karma? In the song, "Another One Bites the Dust," Spiderman Allen mentions that the Super Bowl will be played in New Orleans, after the 1980 season, when he wrote it. And where will the 2025 Super Bowl be played, following the 2024 NFL campaign?

Indeed, it is the Crescent City… New Orleans.

If you are listening, Bobby Layne, let me say this to you: *I have never been a believer of spells, a curse, etc. However, this affliction that has coursed my veins for a lifetime, must stop, and truly makes me ponder whether or not a greater force IS actually at work. The 2023 NFC Championship Game, and the fashion in which the Lions disintegrated, left a mental scar that will always remain. It leaves me contemplating if a Super Bowl will ever happen. The opportunity that was there that evening, often fails to present itself a second time.*

To my Lions soul, it remains ruinous. Your alleged warning is renowned. Again, we are well past 50 years. Allow me to characterize your time frame, as a punt. With the 50 yards (years) "in the air" and another 16 with a bounce and roll, you certainly have us pinned deep in our own territory, while dropping a 66-year "bomb." By any metric or method, we continue to feel the lasting effects of your "promise," which continues to plague us. Enough, sir. Please relent, just once. . .

Endnotes

1   "Bobby Layne," *Wikipedia*, last modified December 12, 2024, https://en.wikipedia.org/wiki/Bobby_Layne.

2   Scott Neville, "Pirates Manager Explains Why He Pulled Paul Skenes From No-Hitter," *Sports Illustrated*, accessed December 5, 2024, https://www.si.com/mlb/pirates-manager-explains-why-pull-paul-skenes-no-hitter.

3   Michael Rosenberg, "Ravens Assistant Joe Cullen's Road to Redemption Began at a Wendy's," *Sports Illustrated*, October 10, 2018, https://www.si.com/nfl/2018/10/10/joe-cullen-baltimore-ravens-coach-dui-arrest-detroit-lions-alcoholism-recovery-naked-wendys-comeback.

4   Michael Rosenberg, "Ravens Assistant Joe Cullen's Road to Redemption Began at a Wendy's," *Sports Illustrated*, October 10, 2018, https://www.si.com/nfl/2018/10/10/joe-cullen-baltimore-ravens-coach-dui-arrest-detroit-lions-alcoholism-recovery-naked-wendys-comeback.

5   Sean Yuille, "John Kitna, Mike Furrey, and Some Halloween Fun," *Pride of Detroit*, October 31, 2007, https://www.prideofdetroit.com/2007/10/31/05312/660.

6   Jenny Vrentas, Joe Cullen's Road Back: Ravens Coach on His DUI Arrest, Alcoholism Recovery, and Naked Wendy's Incident," Sports Illustrated, October 10, 2018, accessed December 29, 2024, https://www.si.com/nfl/2018/10/10/joe-cullen-baltimore-ravens-coachdui-arrest-detroit-lions-alcoholism-recovery-naked-wendys-comeback.

7   "Reggie Rogers," *Wikipedia*, last modified November 6, 2024, https://en.wikipedia.org/wiki/Reggie_Rogers.

8   Dave Birkett, "Titus Young Sentenced to Probation," *Detroit Free Press*, May 5, 2015, https://www.freep.com/story/sports/nfl/lions/2015/05/05/titus-young-sentenced-probation/26938543/.

9   "Titus Young," *Wikipedia*, last modified September 30, 2024, https://en.wikipedia.org/wiki/Titus_Young.

10   "Titus Young," *Wikipedia*, last modified September 30, 2024, https://en.wikipedia.org/wiki/Titus_Young.

11   "Titus Young," *Wikipedia*, last modified September 30, 2024, https://en.wikipedia.org/wiki/Titus_Young.

12   Pro Football History, "What Happened to Charles Rogers?" *Pro Football History*, accessed December 3, 2024, https://www.profootballhistory.com/what-happened-to-charles-rogers/.

13   "Interview: ESPN's Jemele Hill Talks About Her Favorite Athletes and the Challenges of Covering Sports," *MLive*, August 2009, https://www.mlive.com/its-just-sports/2009/08/interview_espns_jemele_hill_ta.html.

14   "Interview: ESPN's Jemele Hill Talks About Her Favorite Athletes and the Challenges of Covering Sports," *MLive*, August 2009, https://www.mlive.com/its-just-sports/2009/08/interview_espns_jemele_hill_ta.html.

15   Mike O'Hara, "O'Hara: Darryl Rogers' Quick Wit is Remembered," *Detroit Lions*, July 12, 2018, https://www.detroitlions.com.

16   "Is the insanity that goes with coaching the Detroit Lions about to claim Jim Schwartz?," *MLive*, December 14, 2009, https://www.mlive.com.

17   "Is the insanity that goes with coaching the Detroit Lions about to claim Jim Schwartz?," *MLive*, December 14, 2009, https://www.mlive.com.

18   "Pride Of Detroit," "Marty Mornhinweg Talks About Taking the Wind," *Pride of Detroit*, June 20, 2007, https://www.prideofdetroit.com/2007/6/20/235816/387.

19   The Four Tops, "It's the Same Old Song," *Four Tops' Second Album* (Motown Records, 1965), accessed December 29, 2024, https://youtu.be/-iMYUZvQtE8?si=4iq35UQYgvMXkcWE.

20   Styx, "The Best of Times," *Paradise Theatre* (A&M Records, 1981), accessed December 29, 2024, https://youtu.be/_fzJGxpcenc?si=qjKFNfkFWLxAV2rm.

21   Queen, "Another One Bites the Dust," *The Game* (EMI Records, 1980), accessed December 29, 2024, https://youtu.be/rY0WxgSXdEE?si=PFiJI7NQldJa6b78.

22 Bob Christoff, "Detroit Lions Silver Rush Anchor Doug English Almost Wasn't," *Vintage Detroit*, accessed December 29, 2024, https://www.vintagedetroit.com/detroit-lions-silver-rush-anchor-doug-english-almost-wasnt/?srsltid=AfmBOopLUihtSXPhsValsohnKCehW_R8PlUhw_LJL9SM3504ZWLh1vxh.

23 Dave Birkett, "Detroit Lions' Doug English Makes Michigan Sports Hall of Fame," *Detroit Free Press*, February 8, 2015, accessed December 29, 2024, https://www.freep.com/story/sports/nfl/lions/2015/02/08/detroit-lions-doug-english-michigan-sports-hall-fame/23073741/#:~:text=Lions%20fans%20loved%20it%20%E2%80%94%20dancing,the%20NFL%20playoffs%20in%201980.

24 Cyd Zeigler, "Matt Millen Calls Player a Slur," *Outsports*, November 3, 2024, https://www.outsports.com/2024/11/3/4010160/matt-millen-calls-player-a-faggot/.

25 Cyd Zeigler, "Matt Millen Calls Player a Slur," *Outsports*, November 3, 2024, https://www.outsports.com/2024/11/3/4010160/matt-millen-calls-player-a-faggot/.

26 "Matt Millen Apologizes for Calling Ron Jaworski a Polack," *Deadspin*, April 27, 2010, https://deadspin.com/matt-millen-apologizes-for-calling-ron-jaworski-a-pola-5523998/.

27 Don Drysdale, "Report: Matt Millen Says He Warned Detroit Lions Owner William Clay Ford About Taking Job," *Detroit Sports Nation*, March 3, 2019, https://detroitsportsnation.com/report-matt-millen-says-warned-detroit-lions-owner-william-clay-ford-taking-job/ddrysdale/detroit-lions/detroit-lions-news/03/03/2019/201318/.

28 Don Drysdale, "Report: Matt Millen Says He Warned Detroit Lions Owner William Clay Ford About Taking Job," *Detroit Sports Nation*, March 3, 2019, https://detroitsportsnation.com/report-matt-millen-says-warned-detroit-lions-owner-william-clay-ford-taking-job/ddrysdale/detroit-lions/detroit-lions-news/03/03/2019/201318/.

29 Greg Pickel, "Matt Millen Still All Heart: Emotional 'E60' Episode Documents Transplant That Renewed His Life," *PennLive*, March 24, 2019, https://www.pennlive.com/pennstatefootball/2019/03/matt-millen-still-all-heart-emotional-e60-episode-documents-transplant-that-renewed-his-life.html.

30   "Matt Millen Apologizes for Calling Ron Jaworski a Polack," *Deadspin*, April 27, 2010, https://deadspin.com/matt-millen-apologizes-for-calling-ron-jaworski-a-pola-5523998/.

31   "Matt Millen Discovers Whole New Way to Embarrass Himself at the NFL Draft," *MLive*, April 2010, https://www.mlive.com/ottoman-empire/2010/04/matt_millen_discovers_whole_new_way_to_embarrass_himself_at_the_nfl_draft.html.

32   Jim Schwartz, "Bobby Layne Remark by Jim Schwartz Sparks Lions Fans," *MLive*, January 13, 2009, accessed December 29, 2024, https://www.mlive.com/lions/2009/01/bobby_layne_remark_by_jim_schw.html.

33   NFL, "Mic'd Up: Stafford Leads Heroic Comeback Win vs. Browns | Week 11, 2009," *NFL.com*, accessed December 3, 2024, https://www.nfl.com/videos/mic-d-up-stafford-leads-heroic-comeback-win-vs-browns-week-11-2009.

34   NFL, "Mic'd Up: Stafford Leads Heroic Comeback Win vs. Browns | Week 11, 2009," *NFL.com*, accessed December 3, 2024, https://www.nfl.com/videos/mic-d-up-stafford-leads-heroic-comeback-win-vs-browns-week-11-2009.

35   NFL, "Mic'd Up: Stafford Leads Heroic Comeback Win vs. Browns | Week 11, 2009," *NFL.com*, accessed December 3, 2024, https://www.nfl.com/videos/mic-d-up-stafford-leads-heroic-comeback-win-vs-browns-week-11-2009.

36   Robert Snell, "Lions' Matt Patricia Jailed 20 Hours After 1996 Spring Break Sexual Assault Arrest," *The Detroit News*, August 20, 2018, https://www.detroitnews.com/story/sports/nfl/lions/2018/08/20/lions-matt-patricia-jailed-20-hours-after-1996-spring-break-sexual-assault-arrest/1047656002/.

37   Justin Rogers, "Live Updates: Matt Patricia Press Conference," *The Detroit News*, May 10, 2018, accessed December 29, 2024, https://www.detroitnews.com/story/sports/nfl/lions/2018/05/10/live-updates-matt-patricia-press-conference/34756115/.

38   Dave Birkett, "Detroit Lions Coach Matt Patricia Reflects on Tumultuous First Season," *Detroit Free Press*, December 26, 2018, https://www.

freep.com/story/sports/nfl/lions/2018/12/26/detroit-lions-matt-patricia/2416044002/.

39   Dave Birkett, "Lions Coach Matt Patricia Explains Posture During Press Conferences After Reporter Confronts Him," *Detroit Free Press*, November 1, 2018, https://www.freep.com/story/sports/nfl/lions/2018/11/01/detroit-lions-matt-patricia-reporter-posture/1852698002/.

40   Erik Schlitt, "Matt Patricia's Tone-Deaf Response to Detroit Lions' fourth-Quarter Collapse vs. Patriots," *Pride of Detroit*, September 14, 2020, https://www.prideofdetroit.com/2020/9/14/21435416/matt-patricia-tone-deaf-response-detroit-lions-fourth-quarter-malcolm-butler.

41   "Brian Flores Patriots coach sends Malcolm in game MALCOLM GO," *YouTube*, uploaded by Brian Flores, February 5, 2015, https://youtu.be/b4qDHJRP3Ho?si=me8cT90w47i-I0FK.

42   Dave Birkett, "Darius Slay Says Lions' Matt Patricia 'Wasn't a Good Coach' and 'Treated Me Like a Rookie,'" *Detroit Free Press*, March 19, 2020, https://www.freep.com/story/sports/nfl/lions/2020/03/19/detroit-lions-darius-slay-matt-patricia/2881160001/.

43   Michael Rothstein, "Inspired by Dad: How the Detroit Lions Made It into *Ozark*," *ESPN*, October 8, 2021, https://www.espn.com/blog/detroit-lions/post/_/id/36494/inspired-by-dad-how-the-detroit-lions-made-it-into-ozark.

44   "Demographic History of Detroit," *Wikipedia*, last modified November 18, 2024, https://en.wikipedia.org/wiki/Demographic_history_of_Detroit.

45   City of Detroit, *Q2 2023 Economic Indicators Report* (Detroit, April 2024), https://detroitmi.gov/sites/detroitmi.localhost/files/2024-04/Q2%202023%20Economic%20Indicators%20Report.pdf.

46   "2024 NFL Draft Attendance Record Set with More Than 700,000 Fans Attending the Event in Detroit," *NFL.com*, April 29, 2024, accessed December 29, 2024, https://www.nfl.com/news/2024-nfl-draft-attendance-record-set-with-more-than-700-00-fans-attending-the-event-in-detroit.

47   "Little Caesars Arena," *Wikipedia*, last modified December 12, 2024, https://en.wikipedia.org/wiki/Little_Caesars_Arena.

48   John Gallagher, "District Detroit Development Gets New Timeline," *Detroit Free Press*, March 14, 2024, accessed December 29, 2024, https://www.freep.com/story/money/business/2024/03/14/district-detroit-development-new-timeline/72949461007/.

49   John Gallagher, "District Detroit Development Gets New Timeline," *Detroit Free Press*, March 14, 2024, https://www.freep.com/story/money/business/2024/03/14/district-detroit-development-new-timeline/72949461007/.

50   Naked Eyes, "Promises, Promises," official video, uploaded Jul 11, 2017, YouTube video, 3:45, accessed December 28, 2024, https://youtu.be/CJK6yfx9AK4?si=kQwsZ_4LY7xPM329.

51   "Tom Gores," *Wikipedia*, last modified December 12, 2024, https://en.wikipedia.org/wiki/Tom_Gores.

52   Sam Quinn, "Pistons Fire Coach Monty Williams One Season into Record-Setting $78.5 Million Contract," *CBS Sports*, December 12, 2024, https://www.cbssports.com/nba/news/pistons-fire-coach-monty-williams-one-season-into-record-setting-78-5-million-contract/#:~:text=Williams%2C%20who%20was%20hired%20last,a%2028%2Dgame%20losing%20streak.

53   Pistons Talk, YouTube, "Monty Williams on why he took the Detroit Pistons job," *YouTube video*, posted June 17, 2023, accessed December 12, 2024, https://youtu.be/-5Jbshcb_m0?si=EGbD1pN1BrOnkXht.

54   Dave Birkett, "Matt Patricia, Bob Quinn Will Return to Detroit Lions in 2020, Despite Fan Frustration," *Detroit Free Press*, December 17, 2019, https://www.freep.com/story/sports/nfl/lions/2019/12/17/matt-patricia-bob-quinn-detroit-lions-return/2672246001/.

55   Scott Rogust, "Lions Finally Give Calvin Johnson the Treatment He Deserved Since Retirement with Ring of Honor," *FanSided*, December 12, 2024, https://fansided.com/posts/lions-finally-give-calvin-johnson-treatment-he-deserved-since-retirement-ring-of-honor.

56   Mike Florio, "Report: Calvin Johnson Turned Down Lions' Offer of $500,000 a Year for 28 Hours of Work," *NBC Sports*, accessed December 12, 2024, https://www.nbcsports.com/nfl/profootballtalk/rumor-mill/news/report-calvin-johnson-turned-down-lions-offer-of-500000-a-year-

for-28-hours-of-work#:~:text=According%20Dave%20Birkett%20of%20
the,of%20%24100%2C000%20to%20Johnson's%20foundation.

57 "List of Largest Sports Contracts," Wikipedia, last modified December 29, 2024, accessed December 29, 2024, https://en.wikipedia.org/wiki/List_of_largest_sports_contracts.

58 Dave Birkett, "Detroit Lions Had to Hire Dan Campbell. Or He Might Have Bit Sheila Ford Hamp's Kneecaps," *Detroit Free Press*, January 22, 2021, https://www.freep.com/.

59 "Aaron Rodgers Explains How He Left Packers and Joined Jets," *Fox Sports*, accessed December 12, 2024, https://www.foxsports.com/stories/nfl/aaron-rodgers-explains-how-he-left-packers-and-joined-jets.

60 Christopher Kuhagen, "Aaron Rodgers Tells Adam Schefter to 'Lose My Number' in Text Exchange as QB Speaks Out on Pat McAfee Show," *Milwaukee Journal Sentinel*, March 15, 2023, https://www.jsonline.com/story/sports/nfl/packers/2023/03/15/packers-quarterback-aaron-rodgers-tells-adam-schefter-to-lose-my-number-in-text-exchange-pat-mcafee/70013938007/.

61 Lindsey Thiry, "Why the Sean McVay-Jared Goff Partnership Fell Apart for the Los Angeles Rams," *ESPN*, February 1, 2021, https://www.espn.com/nfl/story/_/id/31123122/why-sean-mcvay-jared-goff-partnership-fell-apart-los-angeles-rams.

62 Dave Birkett, "Dan Campbell Willing to Tone Down Aggressiveness," *The Oakland Press*, July 13, 2024, accessed December 29, 2024, https://www.theoaklandpress.com/2024/07/13/dan-campbell-willing-to-tone-down-aggressiveness/.

63 Led Zeppelin, "The Song Remains the Same," *Houses of the Holy* (Atlantic Records, 1973), accessed December 29, 2024, https://youtu.be/MTRgvPrUuU8?si=fB23fo2QtH0PZPvY.

64 "Pat Tillman," *Wikipedia*, last modified December 12, 2024, https://en.wikipedia.org/wiki/Pat_Tillman.

www.ingramcontent.com/pod-product-compliance
Lightning Source LLC
Chambersburg PA
CBHW061648120626
46550CB00003B/869